Post Everything

Luke Haines was born in God's own county of Surrey in 1967. He has recorded five albums with the Auteurs, one album as Baader Meinhof, three albums with Black Box Recorder, one film soundtrack album, fifty individual volumes of *Outsider Music*, and three solo albums. He has appeared on *Top of the Pops* and has been nominated for loads of awards but has won nothing. In 2003 Luke Haines was in *Debrett's People of Today*. He thinks that he is no longer listed in this esteemed publication, as the free copy of the magazine hasn't been delivered for some time. It's not the end of the world. This is his second book. The author is married with one child.

ALSO BY LUKE HAINES

Bad Vibes: Britpop and My Part in Its Downfall

Praise for *Post Everything*

'*Post Everything* is written with such authority that it suggests that Haines has finally found his calling: indeed, it's almost as if he's deliberately sabotaged his career until now to give himself something to write about . . . The book's best sections are concerned with genuine failure . . . He brilliantly describes two years of futile effort, and the true pain of collaborative endeavours . . . But Haines's pain provides our pleasure.'

Matt Thorne, *Independent*

'Haines was always too clever to be a pop star . . . As a writer, though, he's a national treasure-in-waiting, cutting through the pomp with drily hilarious anecdotes. *Post Everything* sums up the silliness of the indie scene perfectly.'

Mail on Sunday

'Rueful and flavourful, his tale of grand designs and deep disappointments trumps the sanitised clichés of the average pop memoir.'

I

'Haines manages to maintain a degree of objectivity and offers us a perspective on the music industry as it turns to dust. It helps that he is funny. Like an articulate but permanently pissed uncle, he's a master of the clever cuss and an enthusiastic employer of the tangential footnote . . . This is an enjoyably smirksome read.'

Time Out

'An utterly disdainful account of the British music industry from the late 1990s to 2005. Written in forthright, expletive-riddled prose, it reads like being regaled in the pub by a brilliantly indiscreet misanthrope . . . Hilarious.'

Metro

'"Must never end up like Bobby Gillespie" It's not a bad strategy for life, and happily one the ferociously talented Luke Haines continues to adhere to in his follow-up to *Bad Vibes*. Resuming from where that excoriatingly brilliant book left off . . . Grimly amusing.'

Word

'Thrilling . . . Against the backdrop of a collapsing music business, the rise of Simon Cowell, reality TV, war, and the great New Labour disappointment, this is that very British of things – a celebration of heroic failure . . . Now that Luke Haines' musical memoirs are complete . . . let's see where he casts his gimlet eye and chooses to let his pen run next.'

NME, Book of the Week

'The second coruscating music memoir from Luke Haines . . . It's as funny and scathing as Haines' first book, *Bad Vibes* . . . with a more surrealist sense of weirdness . . . A lot of fun.'

Big Issue

'Haines is still filled with snark and insight, which makes for a dark but enjoyable read.'

Elle

'Delightfully scathing, frequently hilarious dissection of his splendidly non-commercial musical career . . . This is essential reading for old and jaded music fans.'

Irish News

'Luke Haines: genius. I'm pretty sure he'd hate being called a genius, while secretly thinking, Yes, I am one. He is one . . . Scabrous, cynical, self-aware to the point of self-laceration and yet utterly arrogant and inadvertently self-aggrandising . . . Bloated with *bons mots*, acute skewerings ("the Colonel Kurtz of the Curly Wurly Memorial Club, the Shoko Asahara of the Spangles Appreciation Society" – he's talking about my close personal showbiz friend Stuart Maconie) and sly observations (that John Humphrys so despises "Pop Music" he feels the need to add a question mark to *both* words when using the phrase on the *Today* programme: "Pop? Music?"). You will rattle through it . . . In among all the bleating and pissing and moaning, Haines actually proves an astute observer of what's going down . . . While other writers are driven by the tyranny of balance, or the politics of growth, Haines cuts through the shit. He errs on the side of grumpy, but when your author is falling in love, getting married and having a baby, you know that there beats a soppy heart within, and if anything, it makes you admire his jaundiced stance all the more . . . His prose flies . . . *Post Everything* is worth your while.'

Andrew Collins

Post Everything

Outsider Rock and Roll
1997–2005

LUKE HAINES

WINDMILL BOOKS

Published by Windmill Books 2012

4 6 8 10 9 7 5

This book is substantially a work of non-fiction based on the life, experiences and recollections of the author. In some limited cases names of people/places/dates and the detail of events have been changed solely to protect the privacy of others.

First published in Great Britain in 2011 by William Heinemann

Windmill Books
The Random House Group Limited
20 Vauxhall Bridge Road, London SW1V 2SA

Addresses for companies within The Random House Group Limited can be found at: www.randomhouse.co.uk/offices.htm

The Random House Group Limited Reg. No. 954009

www.randomhouse.co.uk

A CIP catalogue record for this book
is available from the British Library

ISBN 9780099537496

Printed and bound by Clays Ltd, St Ives PLC

For S & F.

Contents

Introduction

My first book, *Bad Vibes: Britpop and My Part in Its Downfall*, ends in 1997 with me teetering on the precipice of mental ruin. For the rest of the country this is a brief period of optimism and inclusion; after 18 years of Conservative government the British public have voted themselves 'in'. I have been voted 'out'. Three years before reality television bites and I am already ahead of the game. Never mind, the margins are good. No-man's-land is all right. It's easy to laugh when you're on the outside – and I rarely take the easy option – but just this once please forgive me; after all, being on the outside is what this book, *Post Everything*, is about.

After the commercial and critical success of Black Box Recorder's second album I backed away from the edge of 'the fantasy'. It was the second or third time that I had grasped the nettle – but this time, with no small amount of self-knowledge, I let go. Most of the 'action' in *Post*

Everything takes place in London; I had by the end of the century pretty much extricated the act of 'touring' from my life (Black Box Recorder over a period of six years probably played no more than 20 gigs). This book is about self-imposed exile on the fringes of the 'music scene', and sometimes even further out than that . . .

I still manage to have about five feuds a year. As a man in his early forties I no longer wear each feud as a badge of honour. I am in fact mildly embarrassed by these skirmishes. Many of the deposed of *Bad Vibes* have gone, and in this book there are many ghosts, and despite what they try and tell you, rock music itself, in the 'Post Everything' age is a spectre.

First, a little scene-setting: Britain in the late 1990s. Post Britpop. The dawn of the rock 'n' roll apocalypse. *Post Everything*. If it feels like there's nothing new under the sun, that's because there is nothing new under the sun. The 50s and 60s marked the end of post-war austerity and the beginning of cultural enlightenment. The 70s ushered in the first true age of rock, as well as its first self-conscious year zero – and by the 80s depression, ennui, and irony tumbled over each other to create an accelerated culture. At the turn of the new decade, brass bands and morris dancers were more subversive than rock music. The only way forward was to pretend that nothing mattered. (Everything mattered?) After the death of Kurt Cobain popular culture entered, and is still in, its final phase: Post Everything – where the phones don't ring any more and conversation is silent. Post nostalgia, post reason, post memory – memory replaced by a collective memory for an age that did not exist; we can all pretend to remember communally that episode of *Bergerac* that we didn't watch – y'know, the one where Liza Goddard didn't give old Jim that filthy am-I-or-am-I-not look before she failed to fall through the trap door. Post rock. Post *Top of the Pops*, post Gary Glitter, post the charts, post hit singles, post pop, post modern, post irony, post David Bowie ever making another album. Post albums, post archives, post hard copy, pre-ephemera. Post (real) fame, post real celebrity, post Warhol, Post. Any. Fucking. Good. Post film, post telly, post millennium madness; pre-millennial mumbo jumbo, post millennial mumbo jumbo, post God, post science – does rationalism have to be so damned anti-poetic? (I mean, Richard Dawkins isn't exactly Voltaire.) Post literature – post pens, post paper, post ink, post letter writing. Post romantic – what was your last romantic gesture? Post London – young couples with children leave the big city, the countryside groans with the strain, man, it's like the fucking blitz. Post class system – leisurewear for the new white trash. Post fucking shoes, post leather uppers, post style – wear a good suit well and it can hide a multitude of sins, but don't let a suit wear you. Post suits. Post hats apart from weddings and funerals. Post comedy – Bill Hicks has got a lot to answer for. Post imagination – try taking a surrealistic leap of the mind. Post. Avant. Garde. Post shock – comedians tell rape jokes, M. McCann jokes, wife-beating jokes and paedophile jokes under the auspices of saying the unsayable, safe in the knowledge that the aforementioned won't or cannot make themselves known. But post-political-correctness race jokes are still a no-go area – there may be foreigners in the audience, you might get lamped. Post child catcher, post flashers – what happened to all those harmless old perverts who used to lurk in parks and under railway bridges? Post starving for your art – real artists are just compelled, regardless of whether there is any fiscal demand. They just get on with it, it's a curse, y'know? Post art. Banksy, fucking Banksy telling you what you already know. Post drinking – what exactly is binge drinking? Has everyone forgotten we are a northern European country? Post geography. Post smoke-filled pubs; pre health consciousness, interesting people used to smoke cigarettes. It's getting hard to be interesting. Post interesting. Post fags, post drugs – the older generation, though barely acknowledged, look on aghast at the younger generation's casual acquaintance with altered states. Post old people. Post AIDS. Post Labour, post Tory, post right wing, post left wing. Speaking of angels, where did all the Hell's Angels go? Post national mourning. Post intelligence – human intelligence isn't what it used to be, according to a survey that no one took part in. Military intelligence isn't what it used to be either, according to a dossier that everyone ignored. Post all's fair in love and war. Post world war veterans. Post birth, post generation gaps – where did all the Teddy boys go? Post teenage, post 20-something, post 30-something, post life begins at 40, post middle age, post midlife crisis, post old age – total inability to accept the ageing process. Post age. Post death. Post apocalypse. I'm going to go bleeding postal any moment now – Post. Everything.

Prologue:

Avant-Garde Arthur Scargill

July 2001. What if . . . there was no more rock music? Just as a temporary measure. What if all those lazyboned, hungover dunce musicians just for once went with how they felt and announced that 'This week we are just too un-together to get it together and we won't be going on tour/recording a new elpee/writing another sodding song and trying to flog it to an uninterested nation on breakfast TV.' Sure, I know rock stars do a lot of this 'unable to get it together' stuff, but what if they were just 'too un-together to get it together' ALL TOGETHER? Can you dig? What if Britain's most useless, spoilt, vacuous, drug-addled, slothful, and pointless people went on strike? I'm not talking about the post office, I'm talking about the fucking pop stars. Pop stars on strike. *But striking for what?* chirrups the Greek chorus of no imagination. *More pay?* No, that would be like one of those lacking-in-all-self-awareness-unintentionally-funny Hollywood screenwriters' strikes. This strike – Pop Strike. *My* strike – will be about silence, a chance to ponder the background soundtrack and ask why that hum must always be there. So if all the silly rock 'n' rollers can be convinced to down tools, then what about all the other costermongers of extraneous noise: brass bands, community choirs, carol singers, buskers, chain gangs, whistling milkmen, the WI and blowhards of the comb and paper. Surely they will all fall into silent line as well? Just a thought.

Manager Charlie and I are in the Virgin Records HQ. I have a ruse, a marketing plan, if you like, for the release of my new solo album, *The Oliver Twist Manifesto.*

'The First National Pop Strike,' says David Boyd, my long-suffering A & R man at Hut Records, aghast at this – the wobbliest of notions – and perhaps even more aghast at how much longer his suffering must continue.

'Yep,' I sharpshoot straight back, coolly staring the record boss guy dead in the eye.

'Let me get this right,' continues The Boyd, 'you want to call the entire music industry out on strike for one week . . .?'

'Pretty much.'

'And part of this strike,' clarifies Dave, 'will involve telling the small amount of people who would normally have rushed out to the shops to buy your album on the week of its release, not to do that?'

'That's right, Dave. That would be part of the deal. We will be telling the small amount of people who would normally have rushed out to the shops to buy my album on the day of its release not to do that. We will also be telling those very same people, in no uncertain terms, that if they do stray outside and do the unthinkable, i.e. buy my fucking album during the week of Pop Strike, they will be scabbing. And who would want to be a scab?'

Fucking. Silence. David Boyd slowly spins around on his chair and begins tapping something into a computer. Perhaps he is tapping the words: 'I have finally realised, after almost eight long years, that Luke Haines is a fucking moron. When can we terminate his contract?' But then the typing stops and The Boyd spins back to face me. He is smiling, and the smile breaks into a laugh.

'It's fucking genius,' says DB, 'let's do it. Fucking Pop Strike.'

Industrial action tends to have a momentum all of its own. The general strike of May '68 in France, the miners' strike in the 80s, and now, in the summer of 2001, the First National Pop Strike. The UK broadsheets (mainly) get it and go with the gag, the *Guardian*, the *Independent*, and the *Telegraph* all run lengthy, overly earnest editorial pieces about it. The London *Evening Standard* and the reliably thick *Q* magazine are slower on the uptake, thinking that Pop Strike has got something to do with wanting to put an end to the burgeoning Simon Cowell, and the less burgeoning Pete Waterman et al, and manufactured pop. Ho hum. All this nonsense culminates in my being asked to talk about the First National Pop Strike on Radio 4's flagship current affairs programme, *Today*. Of course, it's a blast, I am wheeled in after an interview with Margaret Thatcher to face a light grilling from John Humphrys and James Naughtie. Even at this late stage in the game, as far as Radio 4 is concerned pop music has never really existed, so for it to be on strike is even more absurd. Humphrys twitters on pompously about not liking Queen (a rock group) very much, still unable to say the words 'pop music' without adding a question mark and upward inflection after each word: 'Pop? Music?' The poor sod is just baffled that this thing – 'Pop? Music?' – exists without his implicit understanding of it. In Humphrys' head it is still 1962, Elvis has been safely neutered by a spell in the army, Cliff Richard and his Shadows pillage the land like the marauding hun, and in the near distance provincial teens are dancing to the drums of death: Merseybeat. John Humphrys is a man who fears the end of civilisation is nigh and this thing called Pop? Music? might have something to do with it. James Naughtie doesn't fare much better, he doesn't like Queen much either, and has convinced himself that my latest solo album, *The Oliver Twist Manifesto* – a kind of pseudo-hip-hop-pastiche-meta-art-protest-album – which I am covertly trying to promote amidst all this Pop Strike doublespeak, is some kind of cryptic terrorist code, and if he mentions its actual title (*The Oliver Twist Manifesto – Quelle horreur!*) then a sleeper cell of former Angry Brigade urban guerrillas will take it as a cue to unleash bloody mayhem on our capital city. Naughtie, a man not hampered by a lack of self-belief, has decided to rename my album and spends the entire interview referring to *The Oliver Twist Manifesto* as 'The Dickens Manifesto'. Whenever I try to correct him by mentioning the record's actual title (the title that its maker had the temerity to bestow upon it), Naughtie butts in with a worried 'Erm yes, no, "The Dickens Manifesto".' I quite like these two mad old bastards, and in their odd way they rather like the idea of my topsy-turvy Pop Strike, though I do fear somewhat for the state of current affairs broadcasting if they're letting people like me on the *Today* programme.

I bid the crazies adieu and in the summer haze of an early-morning taxi home ponder how I got to become the avant-garde Arthur Scargill, leading the workers in downing tools. It's taken four Auteurs albums, two Black Box Recorder albums, a concept album about terrorism, two solo albums and, most recently, the unthinkable – a hit single – to get here. After the demise of the Auteurs and since the inception of Black Box Recorder I have been edging towards the inside, and now I am about to be flung far outside again. I like it. I just want silence. A tear wells in my eye, but then I snap out of it. This is no time for sentiment. This is the time to harden the fuck up. Soon it will be the week of Pop Strike. On your knees, populace, on your fucking knees.

1

Chas and Dave with a chanteuse

Mid-1997–December 1997. The Auteurs resume their grim march through a post Britpop landscape. In a nearby pub some shape-shifting goes on as Black Box Recorder take on human form and grab a record deal.

Post Everything. Large sections of the chattering classes, the liberal elite and some idiots in the music biz get duped by incoming Prime Minister – not I. On 6 May new British PM voted in. Stays for a long time. Late twentieth-century retardation programme of the Great British Public (begun in earnest the moment that Bono took the stage at Live Aid in 1985) continues apace as the first 'Harry Potter' book gains popularity with adults. Princess Diana killed in a car crash in Paris. Prime Minister manages to convert this into a couple of points – gains even more popularity with adults. New Denim single shelved; it is called 'Summer Smash'. Primal Scream still going strong.

By 1997 the Britpop bubble has burst. D. Albarn wisely turns down an offer to schmooze with the government to be. Dumb and Dumber accept. Gallagher and McGee gulp greedily from the poisoned chalice. What on earth are they thinking of? Britpop politics? Even by rock 'n' roll's idiotic standards this is grizzly stuff. Camden Town doesn't so much resemble the shiny new dawn as Hitler's Berlin after the war, where former cheeky chappie guitar strummers trudge the streets like phantom Wehrmacht officers, looking for a final resting place and one last fix. When you get eaten alive by the music machine it's almost a tragedy. Almost. I could have been one of these broken ghouls, but for two reasons: (a) the music machine didn't like the taste, and (b) I got lucky – I have been granted immunity.

After the *Baader Meinhof* album things were close to breaking point, and in early '97 all is wrong. I am dysfunctional, Alice and I are dysfunctional, and I am about to start making a dysfunctional album by a dysfunctional group who I thought I had disbanded almost a year ago. Hut Records want one more album by the Auteurs. A commercial album. Not *After Murder Park*, not *Baader Meinhof*, but an album with a couple of big hits on it. What can I do? I am without a manager (sacked), and I am without a publishing deal (dropped). David Boyd, my faithful A & R man, is my only ally in the entire music industry.

'You're not ready to make your acoustic singer-songwriter album just yet,' DB tells me. *Oh really, this is news to me.*

'It's still an Auteurs album, even if it's just you and a drum machine.' The penny drops. The Boyd is offering me a lifeline: after the moderate success of The Verve's *A Northern Soul* album – with their string-bothering oath anthems for the simple folk – the powers that be have decided it is my turn. It doesn't take a genius to imagine the A & R meeting, but I give it a go. 'If those dunces from Wigan can knock out a few hits then surely Haines has got it in him. Give him anything he needs, just make sure he comes back with a hit single.'

'There's one more thing,' continues The Boyd ominously – DB never warns me, he never stops me, that's why I truly love him – 'I've got to warn you that I'm gonna be a real asshole with you over this record.' These words don't leave me for several weeks, and will haunt me for the next year. When an A & R man is telling you he's going to be 'a real asshole' you know he's going to be a real asshole.

My immunity from post-wartime Berlin – well, late-90s Camden – arrives in the form of a series of chance meetings and a pub idea brought into fruition: Black Box Recorder. After my *Baader Meinhof* psychic meltdown, I make like a recluse, weary from the sheer bloody stupidity that is touring, and exhausted from the solo act masquerading as a group that was (and apparently still is) the Auteurs. When I do stumble out into the light, I find myself absent-mindedly banging a glockenspiel in a folk group called Balloon. Balloon have already scoffed the only crumbs that the music industry will be prepared to offer them a couple of years ago, and are now going through an extended dance of death, all to the tune of my crappy glockenspiel in front of 50 people in the back room of a London pub. *Tinkle ting ting. Bing bong bing.* I am here at the behest of my record producer friend Phil Vinall. Phil desperately wants to save the punctured Balloon and has the bit clenched firmly between his teeth. As for me, I have no idea what I'm doing: sure Balloon have one fabulous song in their midst – a mini-masterpiece called 'Underneath My Bed' – but what's my role? Am I producing it, am I being altruistic, maybe I'm just eye candy? *Ah, what the fuck, it's better than traipsing across Europe in a fucking splitter bus*, I think as I take my place amongst the walking wounded that make up Balloon's 25-'strong' amorphous line-up.

John Moore, a one-time Jesus and Mary Chainee, sits at one end of the stage, a Black and Decker saw arched between his legs and a fucked violin bow in his hands. Moore is Britain's foremost purveyor of the musical saw – vaudeville-style. With his pencil moustache hovering imperiously above his chops and a moist oily rag drooping from his mouth, this fucker looks more like *Dad's Army* spiv Private Walker than any rock 'n' roll refugee. Moore makes theatrical slashes at the blunt edge of the saw with his bow and the sound of Scooby and Shaggy entering the spooky castle issues forth. *Whoooo whoooo, whoooo, whoooo.* In the vanguard of crushed part-time journos and younger hopefuls is Balloon main man Ian Bickerton. Ian is a powerful singer with an idiosyncratic falsetto, and a sackful of folk-tinged songs, a man steeped in the myth of soul and chanson. Lurking somewhere near the back of the stage is the real deal: 23-year-old Sarah Nixey. If you listen hard enough you can just about make out her cooing background magick. It's a rag, tag, and bobtail mob, that's for sure: *Sod it,* I think to myself, *I've got nowhere else I need to be*, so I let rip with the glockenspiel riff of profound failure. *Ting ting ting. Ping pang ping.*

My time as glock camp commandant doesn't last long, for there is plotting going on in the bunker. John Moore and I, having found ourselves to be dubiously 'likeminded,'[1] are, with the renewed energy of a couple of 15-year-old schoolboys, in the process of launching ourselves on the London music scene as an avant-garde sonic attack duo. Of course, we realise quite soon that avant-garde sonic attack duos are much more fun in theory than in practice; besides, we are far too old (John Moore is an ancient 32, I'm younger) to be making unlistenable records. So we do the dirty on Führer Bickerton, we nick Nixey – his *weisser Engel* – with a promise of the stars, and we become a trio. Black Box Recorder. For Moore and myself it's a get-out-of-jail-free card. The music press will come to dig us big time, describing us as a subversive art house trio, and Sarah as a 'rose between two thorns'. Of course, they're fucking wrong. We're Chas and Dave with a chanteuse.[2]

*

[1] At this point in time my friendship with J. Moore is founded upon our typical suburban lower-middle-class love of the New York Dolls and Lou Reed and little else musically. The real bedrock for our old pals act is of course alcohol and bitterness towards the music industry. That and the fact that when we put our ravaged minds together and actually try hard then we believe ourselves to be a force equal to anyone in the old songwriting caper.

[2] Some of the material in this chapter has been covered briefly in my first book, *Bad Vibes: Britpop and My Part in Its Downfall*. Apart from when I repeat myself deliberately, I have made every effort to avoid repetition. For further reading on Balloon/embryonic BBR see also *Bad Vibes.*

'I intend to shit on a lot of people from a very great height.'

'Yeah, well, I intend to shit on more people than you from an even greater height – let's write a song called "Bring Back Hanging" . . .' Spoken like two gentlemen, gentlemen. This statement of intent, this modus operandi, this bulletin from the alehouse – a sample exchange between John Moore and myself from any time in 1997 – pretty much sums up BBR's mission statement. Our first recording, a weird homage to Shangri Las-style disaster discs, entitled 'Girl Singing in the Wreckage', has been despatched to the hungry griffins of the music industry, and what d'ya know, the griffins like what they hear, but a strange thing keeps on occurring: we attend meetings with labels and they enthuse about our new group, but they won't quite commit, the griffins sense perhaps quite rightly that two thirds of this little enterprise have done a few laps of the track already. Careful griffins.[3] So instead of giving us a record contract we are given 'demo money' to record more material. Demo money. Ahahahaha. No, I beg you to stop, music industry. Your bone-grinding stupidity is crucifying me with laughter. In practice what happens is this: BBR go into a meeting with a major label, they don't sign us, but they do give us some free money – with no commitment to them – to continue recording our album. *Nurse. Hand me my spreadsheet, please.*

[3] Between mid-1997 and October 1997, Black Box Recorder attend so many record company meetings that we become entirely nonchalant. During one summit with a major label a hungover John Moore falls asleep.

Here's how the bulk of Black Box Recorder's debut album, *England Made Me*, is paid for, track by track:

England Made Me

'New Baby Boom'	£1,500	Hut
'It's Only the End of the World'	£1,000	Go Beat
'Child Psychology'	£1,000	Independiente
'Kidnapping an Heiress'		
'Hated Sunday'	£1,000	Island
'Ideal Home'		
'Uptown Top Ranking'		
'Swinging'	£1,500	Chrysalis

'Demo money', for a record company, not so much pissing in the wind as pissing up their own noses.

By October 1997, Black Box Recorder, a 'pub idea', have almost, *almost*, signed to Chrysalis Records.[4] On my thirtieth birthday I sit in the pub flanked by Alice, Barney C. Rockford, and The Cellist, the current line-up of the reheated Auteurs – in 18 months' time I will have little or nothing to do with these three. On the other side are Sarah Nixey and John Moore. Ring out the old, bring in the new. The Auteurs are

[4] Record deals take a long time to finalise, and after a few more months' 'chanting' Black Box Recorder finally sign a deal with Chrysalis in December 1998.

currently rehearsing material for a fourth album that no one in the band, other than perhaps Alice, gives a shit about. I can hardly blame Rockford and The Cellist's indifference; since the last Auteurs album, *After Murder Park* (recorded early 1995, released 1996), these two have been fired and rehired, the group is bogus, and we all know it. The song-writing is pretty laboured too. Every time I come up with a killer tune like 'Future Generation', I then get a block and follow up with some try-too-hard crock of piss. To make matters worse, the American Manager, the very same American Manager who helped shepherd the last Auteurs stateside tour over the precipice into disaster, is now the Manager. How this happened is unimportant, all that needs to be said is that in certain points in a band's career, it doesn't matter who is the manager, as rock 'n' roll is at best a very inexact science. The American Manager has, however, redeemed himself slightly by almost bagging BBR a deal with Chrysalis and brokering an agreement with Hut whereby they will allow me to sign with another label whilst retaining my 'services' when I am recording as the Auteurs or solo. Redemption is never free though, someone always has to pick up the bill, and that someone will be me.

Tinkle tinkle, brinng, brinng. Oh god, the phone is ringing. It's that special time of day when the American Manager calls up to discuss at length what kind of record he thinks the Auteurs should be making.

'The kind of record you need to be making,' the American Manager tells me earnestly and transatlantically over the phone, 'is a shop window record.'

Twenty seconds of silence. Of course, 'a shop window record'. That's where I've been going wrong.

'Anyway,' continues the American Manager somewhat tersely, 'I've got to get on with my chanting', and with that he's off. I get the feeling that I am an obstacle to the American Manager's quest for total enlightenment. My future is in the hands of a man who chants. This is the kind of thing that could get a lesser man down. Om.

I hated being young – my twenties didn't suit me. I can already feel that 30 fits me better. Soon I'll be juggling two major-label record deals. There's work to do in the garden, but if you can't spin a few plates whilst you're riding on the unicycle then you'd better get the fuck out of the circus.

2

Reggae research budget

March–July 1998. Black Box Recorder's debut album, England Made Me, *is released. The front cover features former 'glam rock' bad boy wrestling star Adrian Street in full make-up, lamé, and BacoFoil regalia posing with his coal miner father in a Welsh colliery shaft. The band learn how to form a 'piledriver' and go in search of the elusive hit single. The band call off the search for the elusive hit single.*
Post Everything. First euro coins minted in France in May. Charlton Heston becomes president of the National Rifle Association and in June '98 Geri Halliwell leaves the Spice Girls; media interest in this tantalising event is so intense that Halliwell is 'forced' into hiding. Unfortunately, after a few days the former 'Ginger' Spice comes out of hiding.

My songwriting partner, Black Box Recorder co-worker, and by now great pal, John Moore, is a worried man. He is worried that we – BBR – are going to have a hit single. Our well-meaning A & R man, the marvellously named Gordon Biggins (anagram: Big Gordon's Gin), has decided that we need a back-up plan. Our first single, 'Child Psychology', is not exactly all over the wireless, and Biggins is not going to take it lying down. Somewhere, he thinks, deep within the recesses of our album, *England Made Me*, a hit single is a-lurking. Oh yes, Big Gin has a masterplan. We will follow up the album release by putting out our version of Althea and Donna's classic UK-pop-reggae-lite 'Uptown Top Ranking.'

'We don't want to become a novelty act,' frets John through a window of clarity that shuts as we enter the pub, with every intention of getting hazardously pissed.

March 1998. I am on promotional chores sat opposite an ex-*NME* editor on a radio show playing and reviewing the week's new releases. Sadly, the only thing that is 'dead at radio' is BBR's single.The ex-*NME* editor – unfortunately alive and possibly quite well – is known throughout the entire music industry for his infirm twattery. He has indeed turned this unfortunate character trait into an asset. In the world of music journalism infirm twattery can really help you get on. The ex-*NME* editor is now a big cream bun in the world of magazine publishing, keeping a big twatty eye over a handful of music publications. This is rather like lording it over a bucket of shit. Sure, you can strut around telling the bucket of shit what to do, you can have a tantrum and kick the bucket of shit over. You can even have an affair with your bucket of shit. When it comes to the bucket of shit, you are the boss. But therein lies the problem: it's only a bucket of shit, and you have constructed an empire around it – your time on earth has been wasted, and you may as well end it all right now. Maybe that's why the ex-*NME* editor doesn't like Black Box Recorder's debut single, 'Child Psychology', with it's 'Life is unfair . . . Kill yourself or get over it' chorus. Last week the simpleton slagged our single off on air – at least it got played: he thought it pro-misery and that it was romanticising depression. This week, face to face with me, he's not so sure of himself.

'I was a bit worried when I heard you were coming on the show,' squeaks the ex-*NME* editor amiably in his stupid high-pitched scoutmaster voice; the ex-*NME* editor, born bald, always wearing shorts.

'It's all right,' I say, meaning that it's not all right. Unfortunately, now that the ex-*NME* editor and I sit opposite one another, the usual codes of human decency have kicked in. The idiot goat herder is not so brave. I guess, neither am I.

The media reaction to BBR's first single is textbook 'mixed'. The music press mainly love the record. The radio mainly hates the record. The 'problem' is the chorus. 'Child Psychology' is, of course, a ridiculous choice of single – funereal in pace, with long dreamlike spoken word verses, and a chorus that is never likely to be sung by schoolgirls on the top deck of a bus – unless of course those schoolgirls are from the *Village of the Damned*. What truly perplexes me about some people's reaction to the chorus is their anger.

When the ex-*NME* editor passed judgement on the song he was actually annoyed at what he perceived to be the negative 'message' of the song. I glibly wrote those chorus lines – 'LIU . . . KYOGOI' – as a 'quit whingeing' riposte to John's beautifully written verse vignette, the story of a child getting over its parents' divorce, obviously drawn from experience. I thought I was being unambiguous. Then I realise that some people are only hearing some of the words – life is unfair, kill yourself. The crucial 'or get over it' part is going over people's heads. Maybe I should be worried about a Judas Priest body count, but I'm not. The record bellyflops in at number 79.

Everybody loves Black Box Recorder, everybody apart from the people at the radio, the ex-*NME* editor, and the record-buying public. But the reviews, man, the reviews are unbeatable. Broadsheets cream themselves and style magazines love Sarah (John and I lurk in the background of photographs trying not to upstage the singer with our unique raw beauty). This is all very well but reviews (and of course unique raw beauty) do not sell records. BBR's second single and album title track, 'England Made Me', does even worse than 'Child Psychology'. We manage a hat-trick in June when the album thuds into the 'top' 100 for a nanosecond. We shall have to do the unthinkable: tread the boards and have a hit single. Time for a Big Gordon's Gin.

Black Box Recorder are a band originally conceived to exist only in the alehouses of the British Isles and, if strictly necessary, the recording studio. However, our record label, Chrysalis, has deemed it worthwhile to invoke some ridiculous ancient music industry by-law . . . some nonsense about playing live. We shall, it seems, be flaunting our wares on the live circuit. It is quickly decided that our current line-up – a guitar, a fucking Black and Decker saw, and some vocals – may not be enough to sail us through this egregious chore. We decide that we shall surmount the obstacle by having the oddest rhythm section in the world.

'Oi, Chris, play it like rockers, not fackin' "Lover's Rock". Rockerzz!' roars Punky Tone across the rehearsal room to Chris Wyles, Shakin' Stevens's mystified ex-drummer. The 'new' BBR rhythm section are having a crack at 'Uptown Top Ranking.' Bass strangler Tony, on loan to us from the Buzzcocks ('the fackin' Buzzers') is having an apotheosis of punky/reggae crossover. Chris Wyles isn't. Forty-something Chris shuffles about amiably in a leftover 80s paisley waist-coat with the shell-shocked air of a man who has seen a little too much of life and a little too much of Shakin' Stevens. If you didn't know already that Chris Wyles was Shaky's drummer you could kind of guess. John Moore and I immediately like Punky Tone when we first meet him in a Wardour Street pub accompanied by Glen Matlock, a book about Badfinger, a carrier bag of T. Rex albums, a blizzard of shouty swearing, and a stifling smog of patchouli oil. Tone has maybe ten years on the pair of us, but seems even older. Hair in feather-cut, face like Gary Holton, leather-jacketed, tattooed (none of yer *egg fried rice* nonsense, obviously) and wiry. Tone has flung a low-slung Music Man bass around the world with everyone who's ever been half good; he's also done a fair bit of roadie-ing, giving the heebie-jeebies to many an innocent young band, and swearing all over the world in a Mott the Hoople T-shirt. This fellah is old school, inhabiting a realm that begins sometime around the release of Motörhead's first album (*Motörhead*) and ending when the Pistols split up. Punky Tone, Olympian swearer, and an Olympian Rocker – you wouldn't want to get on the wrong side of Punky Tone, you really wouldn't.

'Me and you dahn the front.' Oh God, he's talking to me. 'Fackin' *Piledriver*!' yells Tone, legs apart, head down, bass slung low in the rock stance that I immediately recognize as the 'piledriver'.

'Fackin' come on,' orders the commander of rock. He's not joking – the correct stance of orthodox rock is everything to a man like Punky Tone. I obey, unenthusiastically lining up next to him, doing my best to replicate the front cover of *Piledriver*, Status Quo's classic 1972 blueprint for mindless shuffle rock. A hairline fracture appears in the ice, Sarah Nixey looks baffled – she wasn't expecting to be in a band with men forming 'piledrivers' all over the fackin' shop – but one thing is for sure – when Punky Tone tells you to form a 'piledriver' with him, you'd better knuckle under and form a fackin' piledriver.

Rock 'n' roll managers come and go like new Doctor Whos. The American Manager, wishing to spend more time with his mantra, has been replaced by Manager Charlie. Manager Charlie is the new Doctor.

'If we're going to make this work, then Luke is going to need a reggae research budget,' says Manager Charlie, off to a flying start.

'How much were you thinking?' counters Mr Biggins.

'A grand should cover it,' says Charlie. Confidently.

'Hmmm . . . OK, just one thing,' worries the Big Gin. 'Luke's not taking the piss, is he?' In 1998 the music industry is still thriving, and record companies dole out money like temazepams on a Glasgow housing estate, and why not? The generation-spanning BBR live line-up is primed and ready to leap into action should the occasion of a hit single require massive amounts of promotion. All we have to do now is head into the studio for a few days and rejig 'Uptown Top Ranking', and the one thing we will definitely need is a Reggae Research Budget.

'Uptown Top Ranking' is, in its original form, a thing of true joy, as any child of the 70s will attest to. By the time BBR finish with the song it sounds like it's been fucked with elephant tranquilliser. Any notion of dreadlock has been replaced by pure dread. We are truly negative alchemists, you bring us sunshine, we give you nihilism. The cover version started off as an afterthought during the *England Made Me* sessions; whilst producer Phil Vinall is mixing an album track, we go off and commandeer a little eight-track recorder. The entire song is constructed in the studio vocal booth. John Moore has brought in a sample of an old recording by rum 70s suave man actor Peter Wyngarde. The Wyngarde sample is from a song called 'Rape' (a rakish comedy skit on sexual assault). The Wyngarde monstrosity goes into the sampler and we slow it way, *way* down, until we hit negative time equity. Christ, this track is slow. Next up is 'The Turn'. Sarah doesn't know Althea and Donna's original, which is perfect; she is also magnificently hungover. Again, perfect. We write out the lyrics – mainly Jamaican patois which we cannot make out – phonetically, and Sarah reads them out into the microphone in one take, with all the enthusiasm of a cash and carry shelf stacker. If schoolgirls won't sing along with our songs on the top deck of the bus, then we will make records that sound like they've been made by a schoolgirl on the bus – a schoolgirl from *The Village of the Damned* of course. Bung on a bit of bass – *lemme wind out me waist* – press record, and catch a few incongruous whoops from Moore, and the track is finished in an hour or so. Man, this record is odd.

So, some six months later, in the summer of 1998, we troop into On-U Sound (where else?) to remix our version of 'Uptown Top Ranking' – a track based on a sample of a song called 'Rape' – with the intention of making it 'a bit more commercial' and saving our sorry selves from the early doors dumper. I have used the Reggae Research Budget well. In all probability I have staved off Damon Albarn's Gorillaz project by about two and a half years. I now own all reggae and dub vinyl in London. There is none left. *Heart of the Congos* by the Congos, *Best Dressed Chicken in Town* by Dr Alimantado, Culture's *Two Sevens Clash*, Augustus Pablo's *Rockers Meets King Tubby's in a Firehouse*, *Jesus Dread* by Yabby You, George Faith's *To be a Lover*, *Studio Kinda Cloudy* and *Picka Dub* by Keith Hudson, Upsetter's *Blackboard Jungle Dub*, *Tappa Zukie in Dub*, in fact 'Any Old Duffer Who Ever Set Foot in Trench-Town in Dub', and of course loads and loads of Big Youth. (I even suggest we do a Big Youth covers EP

– quite properly greeted with howls of laughter by my band mates.) My reggae tastes only cover the 70s. None of your Shabba Ranks round here, sunshine. I strictly roots I think you'll find.

On-U Sound[5] is great: you could record a brass band from Grimsby in that studio and it would come out sounding like Augustus Pablo. Old dub equipment lies around like junk at a car wrecking yard: Echoplex delay units, big fuck-off Mu-tron phasers. I Roy's number is written in felt tip next to a payphone on the wall. What a great idea: *Me riddems ain't dread enough, say wah? Me call I Roy on the telephone, he know what to do.* You get the picture. After a few hours 'the riddems' sound pretty 'dread' to me – actually the track sounds pretty much the same as it did when we first recorded it, but we all liked it like that anyway. We hand over the tapes to the record company and wave goodbye to our dalliance with reggae. We sit tight and await the verdict. Another Big Gordon's Gin anybody?

Court in session, all rise. Gordon Biggins gives Manager Charlie the verdict: Chrysalis are not prepared to spend any more money promoting Black Box Recorder's debut album. They will not be releasing a third single – the remixed 'Uptown Top Ranking' – and it is unlikely they will be contracting a second BBR album, as there is 'not much enthusiasm amongst the company'. (It is also unlikely that the youth clubs of Britain will get to experience the pile-

[5] Parts of what will eventually become the *How I Learned to Love the Bootboys* album are also recorded at On-U.

drivin' Black Box Recorder live extravaganza.) Chrysalis, you see, have had a rethink as to what kind of record label they should be. Apparently, some genius has come up with the ground-breaking idea that they should be a 'pop label'. They will be concentrating on the career of their big pop signing Robbie Williams. They will not be concentrating on the career of Black Box Recorder. To all intents and purposes Black Box Recorder have been dropped. Gordon Biggins, because he feels bad about the way things have worked out, persuades the powers that be to give us a little more demo money, and, with unfathomable record company logic, the powers that be agree. Let's just try and clarify the situation: we have just been given more money to record more material by a record label that has just dropped us. Me neither. Whatever the outcome, the search for the elusive hit single has temporarily been called off. Perhaps this time the Reggae Research Budget just wasn't big enough?

3

Sausage Nuremberg

August–October 1998. Final attempt at recording fourth Auteurs album, How I Learned to Love the Bootboys. *Absinthe interruption, and a vegetarian rock star goes doolally over dinner. Post Everything. Pre-millennial jitters set in with the start of the nefarious late-1990s nostalgia boom. Not so much a TV show, more a doomsday cult. Programmes such as* I Love . . . Everything *feature dribble-brained pundits sharing fond memories of 1970s adverts they were too young to remember. Safety in numbers – if we all share the same collective memory then surely we'll make it to the other side. Clips and cunts. And the monster at the dark heart of this light entertainment social cohesion exercise? The Colonel Kurtz of the Curly Wurly Memorial Club, the Shoko Asahara of the Spangles Appreciation Society: Stuart Maconie.*

Is he being 'a real asshole' yet? David Boyd still wants more, and so extra studio time is booked for the Auteurs in August

1998, for the third sitting of the Auteurs' 'commercial album'. The initial attempt at recording the elpee – at the time a loose concept album about telekinetic children called *ESP Kids* – is abandoned as Black Box Recorder gain momentum. The second attempt ends in July with the bulk of the tracks recorded but with the elusive hit single still most elusive. (It's been a pretty frustrating summer on the elusive hit single front what with the BBR 'Uptown Top Ranking' farrago.) Now The Boyd wants more. This could be problematic as I have no new material to record. Certainly not a hit single, not even a flop single or a b-side to a flop single. Fucking zilch.

Intervention, though not divine, arrives on cue. In his spare time, of which he has plenty, John Moore has taken it upon himself to become the UK's first importer of absinthe, deadly green goo liqueur straight outta the Czech Republic. On the eve of the Auteurs' quite possibly barren recording session I stop by Moore's Little Venice flat. Although we don't initially get on, absinthe and I warm to one another. I leave the fucking flat with a broken arm. I take some consolation that although I am the Green Fairy's first new victim, at least this disgusting cough syrup may do some real damage to the chattering public school cunts who will soon be coughing up 60-odd sovs for a bottle of bona fide Bohemia. The arm breakage, however, turns out to be a blessing – in the six weeks it takes for the fucked bone to mend I manage to write a few decent songs: 'Get Wrecked at Home' (what I do when I'm not in a studio or getting wrecked outside) and a cheeky steal of the Rubettes'

1974 bubblegum masterpiece 'Sugar Baby Love' which I bash out on a glockenspiel using my one good arm. The 'Sugar Baby Love' steal becomes 'The Rubettes', an orthodox glam stomper, partly about the tedious late-90s Stalinised nostalgia boom. This bovver beat classic is initially conceived as a Black Box Recorder song, but my/the Auteurs' needs are greater, and 'The Rubettes', co-written with John Moore, may just be the pop gold in the hills.

RAK studios, St John's Wood, London, October 1998. Mickie Most – owner of RAK studios – settles down on a music biz standard issue leather chaise-longue. When the legendary producer of Alvin S., David E., and my childhood fave, Suzie Q, isn't strutting around in a slightly rum leather trousers and vest combo, he busies himself by intently viewing and re-viewing some sort of 'teach yourself to get a pilot's licence' video. The rescheduled recording session of 'The Rubettes' has been going smoothly. It's evening mealtime at the studio, and into the communal dining room slouches Chrissie Hynde. The Pretenders are perpetrating a new album in one or other of the studios in the RAK townhouse. Soon she will be very cross. Tonight, Hynde's ire is about to be stoked up a few notches beyond the bog standard mardiness of the terminally famous, you know, been a household name for a long time, thought that a bit of fame would be nice when young, but now a kind of soggy, loopy confusion has bedded in. Actually, the lead singer out of the Pretenders is going to be furious. Furious with a plate of sausages. My sausages.

For the duration of the recordings of the Auteurs'

'commercial album' (soon, very soon, to become *How I Learned to Love the Bootboys*) I have maintained a kind of neo-skinhead look: suede-head hair crop, green Harrington jacket, and grey Sta-Prest trousers. One of the disadvantages of recording in large established studios is the close proximity of other bands, who are in even closer proximity over the dreaded shared evening meal. Hynde, by now only a few feet away across the dinner table, has declared psychic war on my plate of sausages – staring daggers at my bangers, the avenger of innocent pork death wrinkles her nose like an angry rock 'n' roll wasp, and then turns her gaze upon me.

'I didn't know the Nazi party were making an album,' she sneers at me. Hmmm, I am a little taken aback. I cast my mind back to all the Jews and homosexuals I have slaughtered in the past. The disabled people I have performed pointless genetic experiments upon . . . nope. Nothing. Surely I would have remembered my genocidal tendencies. Then I realise I must be thinking of someone else. Perhaps the lead singer of the Pretenders is thinking of someone else? I'm pretty certain I wasn't at the Wannsee Conference of 1942 when the Final Solution of the Jewish Problem was instituted, and I've definitely never set foot in 'Das braune Haus'. If you're reading this and you're a rock star (or you plan on becoming a rock star), here's some friendly advice: don't accuse someone you don't know and have not even been introduced to of being a 'Nazi' over dinner. It's a really dumb thing to do. Remember, rock stars become rock stars because they are inveterate insecure attention-seeking babies and you may have written a couple of half-decent couplets and memorable tunes, amidst the doggerel and mud, and you really should be grateful that the public bought a couple of your songs in droves, but here's the thing: you do not have to feel guilty, you do not have a higher calling, you just have too much time on your hands. Make more than one album every eight years, try a bit of acting. Alternately you could just remember you are a rock star and shut the fuck up, and please spare us your political insight. The silly vegetarian leans back and turns to her band, upper lip curled like an HRT Elvis and waits for the gales of laughter that will surely greet her searing witticism, but Hurricane Laughter Girdle never arrives, there's just a cold front across the dinner table as the other members of the Pretenders pretend not to be mortified. We all keep our heads down and do a bit of serious chewing as a very long 30 seconds elapses. I eventually break rank.

'Would you be so kind as to pass the bread?' I say, with my best English table manners, but the sentence is left hanging in the air. The angry rock 'n' roll wasp has buzzed off. The free world can sleep safely, fascism has once again been defeated single-handed by a rock star. The rock 'n' roll Nuremberg trials of October 1998 are over.

4

'Glenn, are you thick?'

February 1999. Black Box Recorder have a night out with England football manager Glenn Hoddle, and the fourth Auteurs album, How I Learned to Love the Bootboys, *is at last deemed by the powers that be to be suitable for the ears of the general public.*

Post Everything. The final year of the twentieth century has a bad reputation in terms of popular music. Sure, it's not as cataclysmic as 1955, not as era-defining as the golden age of British beat pop 1964–66. Not as celebrated as 1969, the final year of the strangest decade of the modern age, not even as blamed as 1975 – c'mon, the year that Kiss Alive *was released can't be all bad – obviously not as lauded as scorched earth 1976, and not as self-consciously acclaimed as the post punk year zero, 1978. 1999 is in fact no worse than any year in the 1990s for two very good reasons: 1. The Verve split up. 2. And I release another record so what's the problem? Iris Murdoch dies in Oxford on 8 February, and safe in the knowledge that his legacy will live on, Tony Ainsley, Hull's 'singing butcher' who found fame on Britain's first reality/talent show,* What Makes a Star, *in 1958, passes away. Tony won't be spinning in his grave, for in the new century light entertainment will never die.*

The DATs[6] of the final Auteurs album, *How I Learned to Love the Bootboys*, have landed upon the desk of David Boyd. The Boyd has had a listen and is satisfied with what he has heard. He will not be requesting any more reruns. The awkward gestation of this fucking record is finally over. My relationship with Alice is also over. My expectations for the forthcoming Auteurs single ('The Rubettes') and album are not exactly through the roof. More excitingly, Black Box Recorder have just lured Nude Records (via Sony) into signing us. I'm on my third major label in just under 18 months. John Moore and I have spent the early part of the last year of the twentieth century writing and recording – all paid for by 'demo money' – what will become BBR's second and best album, *The Facts of Life*. When we're not in the studio we use our time wisely.

'Turn on the news now,' yelps John Moore, down the other end of the fucking blower, in a state of advanced excitement, 'Glenn Hoddle is going to resign, you've got to get over here right away.'

'I'll see you in half an hour,' I shoot back, with the clarity

[6]Throughout the 80s and 90s studio recordings are usually mastered on to digital audio tape. Clunky, cheap, and far less reliable than the previous standard of ¼-inch analogue tape. By the twenty-first century DAT will be obsolete, replaced by the virtual ephemera of WAV and MP files.

of purpose of a Mossad agent called into action. Moments later I am in a cab bound for Old Moore's West London pad. Time is of the essence, we must work quickly. You may wonder what the resignation of the England football manager has to do with me. It has everything to do with me. Most importantly, on a misty weekday afternoon in early 1999 it represents an opportunity to get apocalyptically hammered.

Glenn Hoddle has been thinking outside the box. In a recent newspaper interview the England manager has gone a little off-piste – he is now feeling as sick as a parrot. Hoddle has decided to share his views on reincarnation.[7] As we all know when sportsmen – much like pop stars[8] – talk about anything other than their chosen profession, they invariably end up coming across like utter morons. Glenn Hoddle does not disappoint. The England manager has strong views, you see, karma; what goes around comes around, everything happening for a reason, that sort of thing, a mystical dog's dinner for the truly unenlightened. The part of the interview that has scuppered the Hod is his peculiar

[7] From an interview given to *The Times*, 30 January 1999. Go Glenn: 'You and I have been physically given two hands and two legs and half-decent brains. Some people have not been born like that for a reason. The karma is working from another lifetime. I have nothing to hide about that. It is not only people with disabilities. What you sow, you have to reap. You have to look at things that happened in your life and ask why. It comes around.' The Hod had form in the mystic department, when to the barely concealed yet fabulous bemusement of England's more sentient footballers, he hired 'faith healer' Eileen Drewery as part of the national coaching team.

[8] See previous chapter.

belief that disabled people have been dealt their hand as some sort of cosmic punishment for sins committed in a past life. It's offensive as all hell whilst simultaneously being funny as fuck. Poor Glenn, the daft old bugger is so inarticulate he can barely string a few words together without hanging himself. The offending interview was published a week or so ago, and over the days, as the media shit-storm gains momentum, Glenn Hoddle is desperately trying to explain himself – and digging himself further into a hole. Never has one man uttered the dreaded phrase 'at the end of the day' so many times on British TV.

At the end of the day – 2 February 1999 to be precise – Glenn Hoddle is forced to resign from his position as England football manager, and a press conference is hastily convened to take place at Lancaster Gate Hotel – a stone's throw from John Moore's Little Venice flat. Moore has a plan. We need to stamp our 'personalities' on this momentous historical occasion, what – for all we know – may be one of the key historical events in the twilight of twentieth-century Britain. First we need absinthe. John solemnly begins the ceremony. First a measure of absinthe into each of the two tumblers, a teaspoon of sugar dipped in the absinthe, a little water, then fire. The sugar caramelises dripping into the flaming glass. JM performs the final part of the ceremony – putting out the fire at just the right moment. I am watching a sorcerer at work – the magus invoking ritual magick. We drink, then have another, this time without all the hokem. Life's too short.

Absinthe really does get you there, an almost hallucinogenic high coupled with the violent rush of hard liquor. Really rough hard liquor. My initial sniffiness has gone, I quite like the stuff now – sure its viscous aniseed taste is still disgusting, but only a fool would drink absinthe for the flavour. This ain't fucking cocktail hour. This is the time to get medicated and take the path less travelled. Just as the great artists of the past have sought inspiration in the Green Fairy, now Haines and Moore will follow in their footsteps. Wilde, Verlaine, Rimbaud, Jarry – stand aside. We are two very pissed men and we're heading down to Lancaster Gate to bother the England football manager. Uh huh, yeah.

The press conference is scheduled for five o clock, so at just gone four we begin making our preparations. Moore has decided that it will be best if we masquerade as sports reporters. The bottle of absinthe – which we have almost finished – has sharpened our thinking. What we need is placards. JM gets a piece of card and begins scrawling insults aimed at the bozo Hoddle. Meanwhile I decide that I will confront the England manager with a photograph of himself. I scour a tabloid newspaper for a suitable image. The booze and my mental process are now in occult union. Of course, it's obvious, why couldn't I see it before? What I really need is a *tiny* photograph, one that will be barely visible from more than a few inches away. I find one the size of a half penny and Sellotape it to a lolly stick that Moore has pulled out of a box marked 'Things that may come in useful when harassing an England football manager'. This will be my masterstroke – to confront Glenn Hoddle, shamed manager of English football – with a small photograph of himself.

Nothing less than a tiny mirror of, erm, truth maybe. Whatever the fuck it represents, we two cunts are almost ready. Old Moore hands me a pair of stupid sunglasses and puts a harmonica in his pocket for good measure.

'We got time to stop off for a quick one on the way?' I stupidly ask.

'Of course,' comes the withering reply.

A bunch of men in a lift. Hardened thirsty sports reporters heading up to the conference room of the Lancaster Gate Hotel. Two of these sports reporters are less thirsty than the rest of the press pack. Glenn Hoddle's arrival has been predictably delayed, causing my accomplice and me further delay in the pub drinking brandy, which after the green sludge seems like a sobering black coffee. It isn't, and we are well into extra time. We have travelled beyond enhanced absinthe thought and, frankly, are now in a state of some disrepair. The tiny photograph of Hoddle has now found its way onto my glasses, but this is of no concern to me, as I am mainly trying not to slide down the wall of the crowded lift. The men from the press, who all know each other, are trying not to notice us. Perhaps they fear that they are about to be infiltrated and usurped by a new breed of sports reporter. We stumble out of the lift and there is a commotion. Hoddle has arrived. Moore and I are swept along with the press pack, who, moving as one highly intuitive beast, pounce upon their quarry.

'Glenn . . . Glenn . . . Glenn . . .' shout the hunters before launching themselves at their prey. I have reattached the tiny photo of 'Glenn' to my lolly stick. I brandish it at poor old Glenn and yell out, 'Glenn.' Big Glenn squints to make out Little Glenn bobbing up and down at him on the end of a lolly stick. I have the great man's attention but I have no question. Luckily John Moore, buffered to the outside edges of the angry mob, pipes up with what we all know and simultaneously want to know.

'Glenn, are you thick?' Glenn Hoddle peers uncomprehendingly at the former Jesus and Mary Chain drummer. There are a few laughs from the press pack, who have now realised that they have not been infiltrated by Woodward and Bernstein but just a pair of pissed idiots. The proper sporty questioning will begin when the mob finally corner the hapless Hoddle in the conference hall of the Lancaster Gate Hotel. John and I leave them to it. Even though the now ex-England manager is clearly a plank, it's hard not to feel sorry for him: he just doesn't have the intellect to see why people are upset by his comments. Then again, when you know what Glenn Hoddle knows, you don't really have to answer to anyone. Once again enlivened by our good work, we two intrepid news-hounds repair to a room that, intriguingly, says 'Cocktail Bar' above the entrance. It is from here – this fucking cocktail bar – that we shall hatch our next strategic strike of the evening; this time against the media.

I need a plan, a devilishly good plan. I need to find an escape route from my seat in the boozer onto a seat in a cab. My main enemies: terra firma and my legs. Moore seems to have disappeared. I squint my eyes and fix upon the television above the bar. The ITN ten o'clock news; full of Hoddle twaddle. A reporter stands outside the Lancaster Gate Hotel, in the car park, delivering a bulletin straight to camera, oblivious to the two morons in the background pushing and shoving, having a drunken fight. Ah yes, our strategic strike against the media. It would seem that we stumbled from the cocktail bar at approximately 17.45 hours and wandered into a live outside broadcast on the six o'clock evening news. It's like Blur versus Oasis. Black Box Recorder (two thirds anyway) have made it onto the news, which is now being repeated for the benefit of myself and the other punters inside the alehouse opposite the Lancaster Gate Hotel. This Hoddle-bothering may well be juvenile and loutish in the extreme, but this is how Black Box Recorder operate. We are a cipher for modern life, a crystal-making machine. We are drunken miners in the tin pit, we will scrape and we will burrow and we will bring out fossils and turn them into song. You've gotta get your inspiration from somewhere, baby, and tonight we have given you our all. Now about that plan; I'm as drunk as a cunt and I really need a fucking cab.

5

Lost mojo

May–October 1999. Riding shotgun with Johnny Clarke and the Absinthe Friends on a coach to Devon. Auteurs no-man's-land in France, and a dirty weekend in Margate.
Post Everything. Solar eclipse in Europe and Asia on 11 August. In celebration of this natural wonder, One Flew Over the Cuckoo's Nest *author Ken Kesey and his ageing Merry Pranksters travel to Cornwall to get a better view. He is joined by John Moore, apparently. I stay in bed. On 19 October the music business is rocked to its foundations when Billie releases her seminal* Honey to the B *album. Tracey Emin's Bed* (My Bed) *does not win the Turner Prize – I make her an offer (£20k) to take it off her hands. She turns me down. In November hero of many a 70s childhood Gary Glitter is sentenced to four months' imprisonment for downloading thousands of images of child pornography.*

Siân is my type, entirely my type, like no one else I have ever met, or ever will meet. I say her name out loud to myself and it keeps me alive. We are what other people would call 'soul mates'. I first get to know Siân when Black Box Recorder play a small show in Devon at the grandly titled Broomhill Literary Festival. It's not really a literary festival: it's a bacchanalian weekend, organised by John Moore's rather irritating absinthe business partners – the Absinthe Friends, a cocky bunch of brown-brogue-wearing hoorays, all educated beyond their intelligence. The Absinthe Friends see themselves as modern-day flâneurs, idlers and Bohemians. I see them as jumped-up events organisers. I wouldn't have bothered but, after much persuasion from J. Moore, Sarah Nixey and I find ourselves on a rainy day in late May, with the Absinthe Friends and their pet Bohemians, on board a chartered coach bound for the West Country. Of course, it's a fucking blast; on the journey Great Train Robber Bruce Reynolds regales as with tales of safecracking, John Cooper Clarke dazzles us with jokes, and Damien Hirst wanders round like a wounded buffalo, effortlessly proving that material riches do not necessarily make you a charmer. Over three days a sea of absinthe is sunk, the hoorays (and Hirst of course) try to throw a few punches. Debauchery goes on. I could tell you tales but . . . none of that matters, because Siân (who is here to write a piece for a magazine) and I are drawn into each other's gravitational pull, and by the end of the Broomhill Literary Festival we are talking the dawn in on pills and stolen fucking whisky in a hotel garden while Siân's boyfriend, the soon to be editor of *Mojo* magazine, loses his mojo, in a massive cob, listening in to our flirtatious chat from his lonely room up above on the first floor.[9]

By the late summer of 1999 Siân and I are inseparable, demonstrative and in all probability massively annoying to anyone who dares to come within our orbit. There are things which could be terrific obstacles to our union – she is, say it with hushed dread, a music journalist. A fucking music journalist – that most famously failed before you've even begun of occupations. I, on the other hand, am a mentalist minor rock star, so we're even? No, no, no, I always outrank music journalists. Never mind, all things are surmountable for a terror couple like us. I have already defended Siân's honour against some oily bones reporter, a slime bucket of almost outrageous cowardice who fittingly goes under the name of Higginthbottom. When this cunt gets a little over-familiar with my future wife I split the fucker's lip and run him out of town sharpish. Last seen catching a flight to New York, never to return. By the autumn I have pretty much installed myself in Siân's huge rented house in Tufnell Park. The place is a shithole dive of epic proportions, disgusting sick pigeons share our water tank, and no one washes up for fear of what may lurk. It is no place for a man in his thirties to live. It is no place for anyone to live, but I don't care. I feel like I am 18 again. Everything is easy when you're in love, and, man, are we in love.

[9] From this point, perhaps unsurprisingly, I receive almost no coverage in *Mojo* magazine. At the time of writing this same editor is still in place at aforementioned mag. I am persona non grata. All's fair in love and war.

Just as I am enjoying my teenage renaissance I am also enjoying my obscurity. The 'Rubettes' single confirms it is not the pop gold in the hills; as it scrapes into the lower reaches of the chart, the *Bootboys* album does similarly, going AWOL, far down the Nung river, when it is finally released in July, to not many reviews or sales. There is, however, a sense of anticipation for the second BBR album. The only anticipation I have is for the time that Hut Records sever my contract. But they don't. David Boyd has snuck himself an advance tape of BBR's *Facts of Life* album and he thinks it could be the eleventh-hour hit. There is one small problem: for all Black Box Recorder activity, I am signed to Nude Records. As well as sniffing a hit The Boyd can also sniff trouble.

'If it all goes wrong over there [at Nude Records] we'll put the album out for you,' says DB with candour.

Truly the man is a saint. And quite possibly a psychic.

The Auteurs have one more tour to do and then we will be no more. Gone from your lives, you happy ingrates. This time for good. No more reheating the leftovers. I'm out and so are you lot. With Alice gone I've been getting through bass players. Punky Tone helps out for a few shows, but soon he has to go ('Back with the fackin' Buzzers'). So in October 1999 me, Barney C. Rockford, The Cellist, and a new bass player[10] drag ourselves around France for one more short

[10] On 'researching' this book, it would seem that Punky Tone's replacement was so brief and, well, anonymous that no one can remember his name.

lap of dishonour. But wait . . . it's OK. We dash through La République on trains and we arrive at venues and plug in our rented gear and we play professionally to uninterested French people. I remain fairly sober, and we all get on in the way that people in offices who have to work together get on. The only drag is that I am away from Siân. This last tour is distinctly un-rock 'n' roll, no wonder no one likes us. I spend the return journey to Blighty on my own in the smoking carriage, bored of the others' professional company. It's a shame Punky Tone's not here to share an oily with me, extolling the merits of a British Lions[11] b-side and swearing loudly. I'm enjoying this, my outcast-on-the-brink-of-success period. I know the New Year will be full of BBR-ing. Mischief and drunkenness will resume. The train pulls into Waterloo and I bid my co-workers a quick adieu – I won't see much more of them – and dash to be reunited with Siân, who whisks me off to Margate for the weekend. As romantic gestures go it's up there. Margate when we arrive is rain-sodden, windswept and desolate. Fuck Paris, fuck London, and most of all fuck rock 'n' roll. Let's stay in Margate for ever.

[11] See 'Further listening' section at the back of this book.

6

Not entirely dope – the steaming great pile of bullshit and the art of avoiding Mos Def

Late 1999–January 2000. How one thing leads to another. The recording of a film soundtrack, and avoiding a hip-hop summit in New York.

Post Everything. Mentalist TV presenter Richard Madeley is preparing for the imminent Y2K computer virus. On ITV's This Morning *daytime television show, Madeley, who describes himself as a 'millennium guru', is advising viewers that in the wake of the Y2K bug they may, come the New Year, face weeks without gas, electricity, and water. The breakdown of these essentials will, according to the TV presenter, plunge the country into a state of anarchy. Madeley's solution is to keep a 'millennium cupboard', where he stores 'non-perishable food items and bottled water', as well as other life-saving items such as 'candles and string'.*

Never say a thing. If you have a good idea keep the fucker to yourself. Just think of all the trouble we could have avoided if we'd just kept it buttoned, just a couple of happy fish flapping around in the shallow water. And for God and Christ's sake never give a record company the impression that you have a good idea. I have just shovelled a steaming great pile of bullshit from my corner of the room onto David Boyd's desk. The Boyd, having spent a large portion of his adult life running and working for record labels, is now carefully and methodically pushing the pile of bullshit back to me with added interest. I have foolishly mentioned that I am digging stuff on the Rawkus record label. Rawkus in late 1999 are hipper than a hip flask on a tramp's hip-op-deprived hip. The sound of the New York City hip-hop underground. Talib Kweli, Mos Def, Pharoahe Monch – Rawkus muthafuckas to a man. My favourite Rawkus muthas are, unfathomably, the High & Mighty. The High & Mighty inhabit a world that means less than zero to me – baseball, hipster pornography, baseball, and did I mention baseball? I am instinctively drawn to it. Throughout much of the idiocy of the Britpop 90s my mind shut like a bivalve, protecting itself from the tidal wave of gunk, but now I am gradually opening up, and boy am I opening up. I've never really had a problem with musical genres co-existing, and I've never been intimidated by the mores of the hipper-than-thou cognoscenti (despite Rawkus's fearsome reputation). The *Baader Meinhof* album after all was just a collision of ideas – sociopath with unhealthy interest in retro-terrorism jams with KC and the Sunshine Band on a wet Tuesday in a Saffron Walden nightclub, and here's the thing: to me *Baader Meinhof* sounds not too many light years apart from – sonically at least – the blessed High & Mighty, whose album *Home Field Advantage* I inflict on everybody I know. Everybody I know responds with a 'It's just a phase you're going through' look and changes the subject. Everyone except David Boyd.

'Why don't we get Dre to produce your new album,' says The Boyd, as if getting Dr Dre, the supremo of high-concept gazillion-selling rap, to actually produce *my* album is merely a formality. I close one eye and cock my head slightly to one side, it's a look that is meant to say 'Don't be absurd, Dave', but The Boyd is in full flow: he is already fantasising about my duet – or whatever it is that rappers do – with Snoop Dogg. It is a strange conversation to be having – perhaps this much-hyped millennium madness is getting to DB. I had not at the beginning of the year been expecting to still be here on Hut Records by the end of the year,[12] let alone talking about my next album – a solo album – which once again the label is willing to drain the coffers for. But two things have changed since the flop of *How I Learned to Love the Bootboys* back in the summer. First, there is the aforementioned and imminent new Black Box Recorder album, which is as sure as a sure thing can be in the music industry (remember, we are people that

[12] I suppose I should be used to this, as I've been expecting to be 'dropped' since about 1994.

jealously guard all crumbs of hope), and secondly there is the film soundtrack which I have just delivered to Boydy, which Boydy has been digging big time. My stock ain't exactly white hot, but it's an improvement on the cold bucket of sick that it has been at points over the last few years. Boyd eventually manages to get a grip, and we hit upon a plan; why not get the High & Mighty to produce my album, or better still, Mos Def, who has just appeared on the latest Scritti Politti album (also on Hut). I leave the record company office as Dave Boyd starts making phone calls to the hip-hop fraternity. Dre, no way. Mos Def, most definitely.

I feel quite benign towards the Auteurs' *Bootboys* album. Despite being roundly ignored by everyone on its initial release it had a couple of saving graces: it allowed me to put the Auteurs' wounded animal to sleep as humanely as possible, unlike my first attempt at euthanasia after the Albini-produced album, which was messy and painful and allowed the maimed beast to escape. The record has also helped land me a film soundtrack writing gig. Over the past few months I have become friendly with Stewart Home, *the writer and artist who sometimes uses long repetitive pornographic sequences for comic conceptual effect and to bolster his word count*. Stewart plays the *Bootboys* album to a film director friend of his, Paul Tickell. What I hear whenever (and it is not often) I play this album is an extremely expensive patchwork quilt. What Paul Tickell hears is the soundtrack to his forthcoming cinematic adaptation of B. S. Johnson's 70s cult novel *Christie Malry's Own*

Double-Entry.[13] The film is rather oddly being billed as a twenty-first-century *Billy Liar*; of course, it is nothing of the sort. What the film is really about is terrorism. Christie Malry is an everyman dead-end office drone, grieving the premature lung cancer death of his mother. Malry takes a night school course in bookkeeping, where he gets inspired by the works of a monk/accountant in Renaissance Italy to take revenge against all those who cross him: the tobacco companies for the death of his ma, a Rolls-Royce that splashes him in the street, the girls who won't fall in love with him. Right on. I really can't think why I have been asked to compose this soundtrack. Christie, the lone terrorist, starts off by key-scratching cars and builds his way up to slaughtering thousands of people when he poisons the water supply of London. Hmmm, terrorism. The early twenty-first century. Can you see what's coming next? Of course not, so initially everybody has high hopes for this film. Luckily, the film producers cannot afford to pay Virgin Records for the rights to license *How I Learned to Love the Bootboys* – the director's original idea – so I get commissioned to write an original soundtrack. Paul Tickell is dry as burnt bones in a sandstorm, and funny with it, so we get on well – despite him being as northern as Geoff Boycott on an open-top bus driving along Blackpool's Golden Mile.

[13] Bryan Stanley Johnson 1933–73. English novelist, experimental film maker, poet and sports journalist. Notable novels include *The Unfortunates* (1969) and *Christie Malry's Own Double-Entry* (1973). Johnson was acclaimed but not widely known during his lifetime. He committed suicide in 1973.

With only a script by established playwright Simon Bent to guide me, I set to work, quickly and on my own. Just like Christie, I am a cell of one.

At the same time as the Christie Malry soundtrack starts looming, I become fascinated by the true story of June and Jennifer Gibbons, identical twins sent to Broadmoor high-security psychiatric hospital. The sisters, of Barbadian descent, end up, in the late 70s, living in Wales, where their father is stationed at an RAF base. Suffering appalling bullying directed at their speech impediments and skin colour, June and Jennifer form a psychic mystic bond, trapped in a can't-live-with-can't-live-without mutual co-dependency; the legend of 'The Silent Twins' is born. The sisters speak to no one but each other and their younger sister Rose. They develop their own secret language, and gradually withdraw from the outside world into their bedroom to act out violent rituals with weirdly named dolls (Carrot Cabbage Winters) and to write and self-publish disturbing fiction. When a friend tells me that the twins used to have sex with boys from the nearby American airbase 'whilst listening to Kim Wilde'[14] I know I've got a song on my hands. So 'Discomania' – named after a book written by Jennifer – becomes the main theme to the soundtrack of *Christie Malry's Own Double-Entry*. Although the song has no bearing on the film's plot, the Silent Twins' isolation is similar to Christie Malry's everyman nihilism. I figure the song's refrain of 'Which one of us killed us . . . which one of us am I' – a direct quote from the

[14] Sadly not true.

twins' Broadmoor diaries – is actually the chorus inside Christie's head. Other songs come quick and clean: 'England, Scotland and Wales', a new national anthem and simultaneously a mission statement for Christie Malry. Best of all though is a sociopathic bit of prole-baiting called 'How to Hate the Working Classes'. It's great to be recording this stuff when I am brain- and heart-burstingly in love. After ten days I emerge from the basement of a cramped East London recording studio, blinking in the December light, with the bulk of the soundtrack for *Christie Malry's Own Double-Entry* completed. I have still not seen a single frame of film footage.

My house in Camden that I so hated during the Britpoppin' 90s stands neglected and empty. In the past few months I have hardly been there, and when I am there I am reminded of things – not by their presence but by their absence – that I would rather not be reminded of. Siân and I spend our first Christmas together in the big house in Tufnell Park. The end of the century passes and the new one begins. The world does not end. With heavy heart Richard Madeley empties the contents of his millennium cupboard. Things look good for the New Year, so as born contrarians Siân and I decide that it will be fun to escape. But first we need an escape route.

My year-end plans to become an odd sort of avant-garde hip-hop artist don't, in the cold light of the New Year of 2000, seem quite as audacious and exciting as they did, er, back in the day. Dr Dre, Mos Def. The thought of me working with these people seems truly preposterous. Quite silly really. Unfortunately, the big sack of bullshit is back in my court and now I am trying to empty it on some other poor fucker's head. The poor fucker's head in question belongs to a man who may or may not be called 'Brian'. I am having a hastily convened meeting in Manager Charlie's West End office at the behest of David Boyd. 'Brian' is here as a prospective producer of my new solo album. 'Brian' may or may not be in the High & Mighty, I have no idea, I couldn't give a fuck who is in the High & Mighty, y'see with the H & M it just ain't a personality thang. The meeting gets off to an awkward start when I offer 'my man' a hand to shake by way of introduction. Hip-hoppers don't shake hands, I gather, but then I don't do high fives. 'Brian' unenthusiastically and rather limply manages to hold my fingers as I introduce myself.

'Bwar,' says the hip-hopster sulkily by way of introduction. I ask once more, and this time get a 'Brer' for my troubles. Okay, 'Brian' it is. I try and make some conversation but it really is a bit of a culture clash that we have here. Me in my suit, 'Brian' in his oversized PE kit and stupid trainers. I decide that the best thing to do in this, or any, situation is give 'Brian' a blast of *Baader Meinhof,* then he will see that just as KC and the Sunshine Band and terror reportage can co-exist together, so then can the NYC hip-hop underground and Luke Michael Haines. The *Baader Meinhof* album spins its lonely circles for a few minutes and 'Brian' delivers his verdict.

'Yeah. Dope.' My god, this is practically a soliloquy. 'Dope,' confirms 'Brian' before switching back to somnambulism cruise control. And that is as good as it gets. Sure, we get a few more 'Dopes' from 'Brian', but soon, and not before time, Manager Charlie brings the awkward hip-hop summit to an awkward end.

'I think that maybe we should get the record company to fly you to New York, you could meet up with Mos Def while you're there,' says Manager Charlie, once 'Brian' has shuffled out of the building. I'm about to tell MC that I don't want to pursue this ridiculous hip-hop thing any longer, when a light goes on in my head.

February 2000. I have two plane tickets in my pocket, one for myself, one for Siân – the record company is flying me out to New York City, where I am to meet with Mos Def to discuss the possibility of his producing my album. I have on my person Mr Def's phone number – arrangements to meet have not yet been finalised. As our taxi hurtles towards Heathrow, 'The Facts of Life' comes on the radio, everything is perfect until some dunce journalist – the very same fucking moron who told me that I had lost out on the Mercury prize by one vote – comes over the airwaves to pronounce her learned opinion on the BBR masterclass.

'Basically, a rip-off of All Saints,' says Madame Plank.

'Arghhh, NO, you dribble-brained administrator of pure cack,' I yell at the stupid radio, 'it's a rip-off of "Honey to the B", by Billie Piper not the fucking All Saints. You cloth-eared, witless cunt.' Ah, when the irony is lost. I ask the cab driver to switch stations. BBR again, we are all over the goddamn radio. I stare out the window at the cars stuck bumper to bumper queuing for Terminal 2. Frustrated drivers scour the wavebands, but resistance is futile, no one can escape the Black Box Recorder Reich of radio domination. *I must make every effort to not meet up with Mos Def*, I think to myself as we arrive at the airport.

We drink our way over the Atlantic – perhaps we drink the Atlantic. I am in love and I have no fear of flying. I raise my glass to the real power of positive drinking. We arrive barely able to stand, clear immigration, and plunge into a New York taxi that will deliver us, stinking drunk but happy, to the SoHo Hotel, where we meet our friend Page Hamilton from US hardcore heroes Helmet for ludicrously expensive cocktails. I must avoid Mos Def – in fact I'm starting to get paranoid and I'm seeing rappers everywhere. It's all right though 'cos Page is Mister Fucking New York City and he can get us the hell out of this cocktail bar and take us spinning through the metropolis.

We awake back in the hotel, our heads still cartwheeling with last night's booze, but by now I am worried: on my way back to the room I think I spot Mos Def in the lobby. Is it a coincidence? Does he know I'm here? Maybe I called him up when I was drunk last night, perhaps I have arranged to meet him right now. When I get to our room on the third floor Siân is taking a shower. I turn on the TV and flick through the endless shit until I stumble upon *Enter the Dragon*, which is nearing its conclusion. I settle down to watch as Bruce Lee stalks Han his mortal enemy through the hall of mirrors. As Lee goes to smash the mirror something strange happens: the face of dead rapper Notorious B.I.G. appears on the TV screen.

'Yo, homies, you ain't got no business here,' says Biggie. I realise that he is talking to me. 'Thing's been good round in tha hood, dig? Niggaz takin' care of their own business, 'til you haul up with your white ass.'

'Biggie is right,' says Bruce Lee from the corner of the TV screen. Oh Christ, I think to myself. It's bad enough that deceased west coast rappers are having a go at me without dead kung fu stars no doubt pitching in with questionable and predictable eastern hokum.

'When the man in the bowler hat can no longer see the dragonfly on the lily, then the song will be over,' continues the star of *Enter the Dragon* and *Fist of Fury*.

'Shee-iit, what the fuck you talking about, Bruce Lee,' says Biggie, but it's too late. Bruce Lee has vanished into the hall of mirrors, once again looking for Han. He has left us with his wisdom. He does not require a reaction.

'Sure, my nigger "Brian" said your iddy-biddy *Baader* whatnot was dope 'an all, but "Brian" sure can be a dumb ass.'

'So, Biggie, are you saying that "Brian" doesn't know what is dope and what is not dope?' I ask of the Notorious B.I.G.

'"Brian"'s a moron,' counters Smalls.

'Look,' I say, appealing to what I hope is the departed rapper's better nature, 'I don't really want to make a hip-hop album, I just quite like the High & Mighty. I gave Dave Boyd my sack of bullshit, he ran with it, and then he gave me his sack of bullshit. I'm just a whitey from Blighty and now I'm in New York City being stalked by rappers, some alive and some, like you, Biggie, who are dead.'

The late Notorious B.I.G. eyes me square on from the set of *Enter the Dragon*. It was a winning speech for sure.

'I don't know nuthin' 'bout no sacks of bullshit, but I can see you got heart for a white man. You just get the fuck outta here, before you end up getting a Tupac tattoo on ya skinny white ass.' And with that the dead legend is gone. *Bitter sod*, I think to myself.

'Maybe we should move to a different hotel,' I say to Siân as she emerges from the shower room.

The Chelsea in Midtown, I figure, will not be plagued with hip-hopsters – alive or otherwise. The only ghosts in the Chelsea Hotel are the ones that have lived there – on a fixed rent – for decades. Back in 1993 on my first visit to Manhattan with the Auteurs, the place still had its share of crazies, but by the end of the 90s Mayor Rudolph Giuliani had cleared New York City of all the bad people, with his blitz on drugs and drug-related crime, and now in early 2000 any lunatics still left from Giuliani's purge have moved into the Chelsea Hotel. The place is practically a living museum to old New York: ancient drag queens stalk through the corridors, witchy women make nightmarish montages out of decapitated children's dollies and stick them on the front of their doors, and at night no one bats an eyelid at the screams coming from the rooms of some of the hotel's more established guests. Siân and I keep our heads down for our last few nights in the city, going with the Chelsea flow.

On the way back to JFK airport I leave Mos Def's phone number in the cab – someone else can use it. This trip has been a fucking blast. I have taken Biggie and Bruce's advice and successfully avoided making a disastrous hip-hop album. I have also avoided appearing in the video for BBR's 'Facts of Life' single, which has been taking place in London during my absence (I strategically timed this excursion to coincide with the video shoot). I return home knowing that a hit single is imminent, but really, by now, that just ain't so important. Siân and I have decided that we should get married. Pronto.

7

Tiny, annoying dog

March–April 2000. Cuntgate.
Post Everything. All Saints' producer, William Orbit, makes maximum use of 'whooshy' pre-chorus effect (see following chapter) on 'Pure Shores', the Saints' last imperial-phase single. Irritating music fan Nick Hornby gets the Hollywood treatment for his irritating twee 'novel' High Fidelity. *Vladimir Putin elected Russian President.*

Saul Galpern is the head of Nude Records – long-time home to Suede and now, in March 2000, home to Black Box Recorder. Saul's other more sinister role is as the owner of Marnie, a very small and very annoying dog. I don't like dogs much. Nasty, gnashing, indiscriminately shitting, wantonly pissing little fuckers. If a dog is man's best friend then humanity is even more fucked than previously thought. My hatred of doggies is mutt-reciprocated. As a tiny tot a rotten Rover detected my nascent canine bad vibes and tried to yank my two-year-old self out of a cot. I survived and the woofer was sent off for a nice long sleep. Me 1, Dogs 0. Marnie, Saul's little furry friend, has also detected my doggie bad vibes and has taken a strong dislike to me. Every time I walk into the record company office I am welcomed by Marnie, growling and yapping at my heels. Saul Galpern, like all deluded dog lovers, is oblivious to his horrible pet's ghastly behaviour, rewarding every snarl of its vicious tiny choppers with a loving chocolate treat. I'd like to throw the fucker out the first-floor window (Marnie not Saul – or perhaps both of them) and perhaps at any other time I would, but right now I figure for everyone's sake it's better if Marnie doesn't go airborne: you see, Black Box Recorder are about to have a hit single.

Galpern is all right. Like David Boyd at Hut Records he is one of the good guys. Saul has been sniffing around me since the early 90s showing an initial interest in the proto Auteurs and now – in the wake of Black Box Recorder being dropped by our former label Chrysalis – has stepped into the breach. Saul is a canny wee Jock: short arms, long pockets, in strict accordance with the laws of ethnic stereotyping. The deal Galpern offers us is cash-light, but fuck it, no other record labels are coughing up. So without too much enthusiasm the three of us, John Moore – my songwriting partner – chanteuse Sarah Nixey, and myself sign on the dotted line with Nude Records. Then something happens: the radio starts playing the title track and first single from our soon to be released second album, *The Facts of Life*. By the end of February we have been added to the Radio 1 C list. OK, fine, let's not get any ideas. A week later we're on the B list. Uh huh, then the A list. Man, I haven't been up in these giddy heights for years.[15] So we get a month's solid daytime airplay before the single's release in April. Try not to fuck it up, eh?

It's a young man's game – rock 'n' roll – or at least it should be; even at the age of 25 at the start of the Auteurs I felt vaguely embarrassed to be in a fucking pop group. *Must never end up like Bobby Gillespie*. Now, at the age of 32, I consider myself entirely decrepit in terms of being in a fucking pop group. My only consolation is that in this fucking pop group I do not have to be the fucking lead singer. I am sat with the lead singer, Sarah Nixey. The Turn and I are stuck in the drab interview room surroundings of our PR company. Bottles of red wine glisten seductively on the table. A small boy from the *NME* sits nervously on the other side of the table. I pour myself a large tumbler of booze, and make a point of not offering any to the reporter. Nixey and I are rather gamely fielding the journo child's barrage of unimaginative yet enthusiastic questions. This will have to stop.

By the end of the 90s as the Britpop era crashed and burned so too did the UK music press. The response to flagging sales is obvious: why not fill the pages of the rock press with interminable lists, and for good measure extract any smidgeon of humour. Job done. Someone else's problem. Right now I am wrestling with a different problem: the path

[15] 'Lenny Valentino', November 1993.

less trodden. The midweek chart position for *The Facts of Life* is number seven. Number fucking seven. Myself and Black Box Recorder are officially *NME*-friendly again. So *NME*-friendly that the rag has despatched a cameraman to film this momentous interview for its website. If only for my own amusement I want to liven up this dreary interrogation. *Yap yap yap*, goes the baby music writer, *pant pant pant*, on and on, like an over-excited puppy at my feet. My thoughts turn darkly to Marnie, my tiny nemesis; the small Saul dog is on my mind, and I'm feeling the need to share.

Having already sunk one bottle of red wine I go to work on number two. The journo asks me a question about our record label. This I decide will be the ideal forum to make known my hatred of Saul Galpern's mutt Marnie; however, the fog of wine is giving me navigational problems. I realise in the nick of time that if I call the dog a 'cunt', I will seem slightly deranged. I have a problem. I have to call someone a 'cunt' so I sidestep the issue.

'Saul Galpern is a cunt,' I blurt out, 'and our record label are cunts.' I realise that this last statement is grammatically confused so I add, 'Everyone at our record label is a cunt', just to assuage any doubt. The boy-child from the *NME* looks aghast. Sarah Nixey, usually inscrutable and unflappable, now looks scrutable and flapped. The silence is only broken by an ashen-faced PR who has entered the room just in time for my state of the nation address.

'You've just been offered *Top of the Pops*,' says the PR weakly.

'Fabulous,' I say as I happily pour myself another large

glass of wine. Within minutes the tiny tot from the *NME* is on the phone to Nude Records gleefully alerting Saul Galpern to the fact that I have just been filmed calling him a 'cunt', and would he like to respond. He would; he says that no one has ever called him a 'cunt' before,[16] and after many years in the music business this is the first time he has felt like giving up. Manager Charlie has also been tipped off. He too mutters something about 'None of this being worth it.' I, on the other hand, am rather pleased with my morning's work. I am unburdened, I've indirectly got the 'Marnie situation' out in the open. Sure there has been collateral damage. My relationship with Marnie may still be 'dysfunctional' – let's face it she would never have known if I had called her a 'cunt', she's just a fucking dog – and so what if I have accidentally called Saul Galpern a 'cunt', albeit in a rather public way. (I would have called him a 'cunt' sooner or later anyway.)

At the age of 32, when some men would be worrying about the loss of youth and the onset of middle age, looking inward for more profound meaning, I too have delved deep; I have learned that I am prepared to throw it all away over my most primal fear: a tiny, annoying dog. Sod hit records, sod *Top of the Pops*, and sod musical differences. When two men fall out over a pet, things will get nasty. Man, you better run for the hills. Final score: Me 2, Dogs 0.

[16] I somewhat doubt this.

8

Pop music is wasted on the young

April 2000. Black Box Recorder storm Top of the Pops. *Post Everything. Clocks mainly stop, as weakened broken nation gather around tragic lanterns to watch Black Box Recorder on* Top of the Pops. *Elsewhere, Brink's-Mat robber Kenneth Noye is sent to prison for the 'road rage' killing of Stephen Cameron by an M25 slip-road. John Moore and Luke Haines are both in attendance at Noye's Old Bailey trial. All Saints and Smashing Pumpkins find time to call it a day.*

Top 20 singles, week ending 15 April 2000:

1. *'Toca's Miracle' – Fragma*
2. *'Fill Me In' – Craig David*
3. *'Thong Song' – Sisqó*
4. *'Flowers' – Sweet Female Attitude*
5. *'The Bad Touch' – The Bloodhound Gang*
6. *'Blow Ya Mind' – Lock an' Load*
7. *'I Wanna Love You Forever' – Jessica Simpson*

8 *'Just Around the Hill' – Sash*
9 *'Never Be the Same Again' – Melanie C/Lisa 'Left Eye' Lopes*
10 *'Deeper Shade of Blue' – Steps*
11 *'A Song for the Lovers' – Ashcroft*
12 *'Say My Name' – Destiny's Child*
13 *'Freaky Time' – Point Break*
14 *'Fool Again' – Westlife*
15 *'Airwave' – Rank 1*
16 *'The Time Is Now' – Moloko*
17 *'Smooth' – Santana*
18 *'Sister' – Sister 2 Sister*
19 *'All the Small Things' – Blink 182*
20 *'The Facts of Life' – Black Box Recorder*

A truly vintage chart.

How the hell did I get here? Well, we rather embarrassingly hired a white stretch provincial hen night limo to pick us up (Black Box Recorder plus entourage) from our favourite boozer, the Spread Eagle in Camden Town, where the landlady and landlord wave us off (we are good customers), then it's straight up the Finchley Road and onto the North Circular Elstree-bound. No. How the hell did I get *here*? The mainstream. The last time I was anywhere near a TV show I got involved in an argument with the producer about disabled rights, a subject I had no interest in before or since or at the time, and the occasion before that . . . well, never mind. Let's just say I am as surprised as anybody else to be here, on a wet Tuesday morning in April at the BBC studios, miming the latest BBR single on *Top of the Pops*. Or am I? Let me tell you a tale of brave and noble men and damsels in distress . . . and *Top of the Pops*.

'The Facts of Life' has settled in at number 20 in the official UK singles chart, proof enough if it were needed – and it is, because this one is a POP record, and that is the point of POP records, to be POP-ular – that we have succeeded in doing what we set out to do: give the world a Scientifically Constructed Hit Record. We might as well enjoy it while it lasts (which won't be for long) *because for you, Black Box Recorder, ze war is over*.

Let's just say, for the sake of context and to make life easy, that the first Black Box Recorder album, *England Made Me*, was a commercial disaster. I thought it had sold pretty well but the record company disagreed. The upshot of this is some unenlightened yet predictable behaviour from our then label, Chrysalis, who 'drop' us a few months after the album's release in mid-'98. For me this is a mere trifling setback: I am still signed to Hut Records (as the Auteurs) and I am still, quite bafflingly, being showered with more money than I know what to do with. For Sarah, our front woman/singer/cipher/persona, the consequences of Chrysalis's lack of foresight are more significant. She has had to, *whisper it*, go back into the 'workplace'. As for John Moore, the 'workplace' is not an option. Whenever money gets tight he seems to have an elaborate yet entirely legal system of compensation schemes to fall back on. Yes, Sarah is the one who is suffering, in this strange and frightening world of 'the workplace'. It's a tragedy and John and I feel more than a twinge of guilt

– after all, we were the ones who dragged Damsel Nixey out of the world of gainful employment, and now at the tender age of 25 she has been cruelly thrown back there. We must act quickly. We are chivalrous Knights of the Realm on a mission to save our sweet maiden. We will lay down our metaphorical coat across the putrid puddle of degradation that is 'the workplace'. Place your dainty foot forwards, dear lady, and step over into our magical land. Sweet chanteuse, if we cannot write a hit single for ourselves, then for all the right reasons we shall write you a Proper Fuck-Off Hit Single.

Hit singles are a tricky-dick business: if they really were a piece of piss even *you* would write one. To write a hit you have to swallow your pride and engage, *really engage*, with the populace. Of course my track record with the populace is slightly tarnished, so the songs about terrorism, suicide, infanticide, self-mutilation et al are out of bounds. Even the Beatles in that hallowed period of the late 60s – when the experimental did briefly swim alongside the mainstream – didn't really cut the apron strings of good old showbiz, with their nursery rhyme ditties ('I Am the Walrus', 'Lady Madonna'), insurrectionist cop-outs ('Revolution'), inanity ('Hello Goodbye'), and songs about voluntary – or otherwise – repatriation ('Get Back').[17] So we make a decision: we'll

[17] The Beatles' political compass was infamously wobbly. It took yer Fabs until 1966 to make a brief statement on the Vietnam war. They were against it. In 1968 John Lennon returned his MBE in protest against Great Britain's involvement in the Biafran war – and more pressingly at the Plastic Ono Band single 'Cold Turkey' slipping down in the charts. The same year saw Lennon record two versions of 'Revolution', unable to decide if he wanted

stick with the classics, or rather the classic: hanky panky, slap and tickle, a bit of how's yer father. Sex.

OK, so we don't entirely engage with the populace, but we have been listening to a bit of Proper Pop Music, and right now I'd rather jack than Fleetwood Mac, as a wise man (or at least the Reynolds Girls) once said. I have become obsessed with TLC and their high concept R & B, also All Saints, a risible bunch of morons whose utter hopelessness – in the care of state-of-the-art ironic retro production – somehow conspires to help them reach greatness. But more important than both TLC and the All Saints is Billie Piper. Billie's 'Honey to the B' is a smokin' hot tune, it's up there

---

'in' or 'out' of any forthcoming insurrectionary shenanigans. On the notorious bootleg of the *Let It Be* sessions known as 'The Black Album', an early version of 'Get Back' appears with the lyric 'don't want no Pakistanis taking other people's jobs'. Other selections include 'Commonwealth' and a blues jam where soft lad McCartney repeats the phrase 'White power' over and over, as Lennon screams back 'Get off'. Beatles apologists are prone to muttering that these recordings were at best clumsy satire, and it is probably best to give them the benefit of the doubt; that said, the 'Black Album' recordings – none of which made it on to the barrel-scraping anthology collections – are a rum listen. It took Lennon until 1972 to make his grand political statement, with the disastrous *Some Time in New York City* album. Lennon may or may not have taken some pleasure in the fact that due to the harassment he was receiving over his immigration status from the Nixon administration, he was the subject of an article in the Black Panther newspaper, the first time the Panthers had ever supported a 'white radical'. Lennon may not have been so pleased that he was named by the paper as the author of 'Give Ireland Back to the Irish', Paul McCartney's helpful commentary on 'The Troubles'. Perhaps to the Black Panthers those whiteys from Blighty all looked the same.

with the greats: Glen Campbell's 'Wichita Lineman', 'Tago Mago' by Can, 'Approximately Infinite Universe' by Yoko, *Metal Box* by PiL, 'Never Ever' by the All Saints. Er, OK, so 'Honey to the B' is something of a 'Never Ever' lite, but this contrivance, like the very existence of the All Saints, somehow elevates Billie Piper into truly over-achieving high art. Either I am starting to love pop music a bit too much or I am turning into Paul Morley. With 'Honey to the B' as our Holy Grail, Moore and I start working on 'The Facts of Life'. We've had the title for a while, then out of my lazy brain a swing-beat-style tune with a killer chorus pops into my head, I quickly bash out a demo, and then, 'inspired' by a 1950s sex ed manual, John Moore comes up with a smart-arse talky-verse lyric. As soon as it's conceived we know that 'The Facts of Life' should be a smash.

BBR's original recording of 'The Facts of Life' is a classic, as of its time as smallpox but great nonetheless. But there's something missing: it has not been produced by Pete Craigie. 'Who is Pete Craigie?' cry the unenlightened hordes. Pete Craigie is only the producer of Billie's 'Honey to the B' and the rest of us are mere mortals. We decide that we must call upon the services of this dark necromancer to remix our pop masterpiece.

Pete Craigie is everything that a Proper Pop Producer should be. Wears flip-flops and shorts in the studio, has a small army of assistants working on other computers to search out the best whooshy-woo noises that are essential to all Proper Pop Music. Probably lives near Maidenhead, probably drives an executive saloon car, and probably doesn't like to work on Sundays when the Formula 1 is on TV. He maybe even has the odd Bar BQ, where he invites the other big pop producers du jour to talk about the current state of computerised recording and the latest developments in F1? We may never know for sure. Like many of the great seers before him, Craigie's art is dark, and the only thing we can say with certainty is that when Pete Craigie has finished weaving his mystic spell, he imbues any recording he touches with that most elusive of qualities – radio friendliness.[18] And man oh man do the radio and our record become friends. From the moment it's out of the box our single becomes fucking omnipresent. I start to feel uneasy. We will soon be on the inside. The inside is bad. Outside is good.

Our new album of the same title, *The Facts of Life*, has mainly been recorded over a stop-start period of six months between the end of 1998 through to the early summer of '99, almost the very point when my own life changed dramatically: after my split with Alice, the end of the Auteurs,

[18] BBR's radio domination during the spring of 2000 is helped in no small part by the DJ double act of Mark Radcliffe and Marc Riley, whose championing of 'The Facts of Life' on their Radio 1 afternoon show ensures us plenty of daytime airplay. At one point during Radcliffe and Riley's weird tenure on Radio 1 they even end up briefly hosting the breakfast show. Let's just put this into perspective: a former member of the Fall (Riley) is presenting the Radio 1 breakfast show. These are strange times. Of course, it cannot last and eventually the duo are smoked out of 'The Nation's Favourite', and Black Box Recorder's chart-bothering goes no further.

the *Christie Malry* film soundtrack, and my imminent marriage. The success of 'The Facts of Life' single and album is a fait accompli. I am so certain of its commercial prowess that I have put it to the back of my mind until now. So this is what it feels like to be firing real bullets.

Sarah Nixey is a born pop star, I think to myself as she steadies herself for a camera rehearsal. I'm glad we made her one, our work is done. I'm also glad that the Auteurs never appeared on *Top of the Pops*: man, we would have blown it big time – it's bad enough now, what with me not talking to the record company over that business with the fucking dog. Our record label, Nude, has despatched a lackey to accompany us to the BBC; at one point the lackey asks me if we can be friends again. Good grief. Not likely, sunshine, do you think I am going to pass up the chance of appearing on *TOTP* whilst simultaneously being at loggerheads with the label? That, my friend, is just not in my script, maybe later, but for now we are at war. Over a small dog. So we do all the things that people who have appeared on *Top of the Pops* do: take the piss out of the other performers, get thrown off the set of *EastEnders* . . . there's not much really to do. The studio is on the shabby side of drab, the cameramen are jobs-worths and the bar is like the railway workers' union, where you wouldn't be at all surprised to see Bob Crow staunchly nursing a pint. But none of this matters, because the thing about *TOTP*, that most shoddily treated British institution, is that it all exists in the imagination of the viewer. So come the time, come the band, we know that when the cameras start to roll, the silver bullet must be a clean shot straight into the public psyche.

Britney has done her thing on the stage sidelong to us. Now it is our turn. The small gaggle of 50 or so young people that pass for an audience are shepherded over to our stage, where they are strategically placed to look like what they are not: an enthusiastic crowd. Our own small entourage, whose ages range from late twenties to late thirties, have been unsubtly ushered to the back of the room, lest they get in camera shot. When this performance is transmitted into the homes of the Great British Public three days later, one illusion will be intact – that Black Box Recorder are a big hit with the teens. No matter, we give it our best shot. BBR in their imperial phase. I do my best straight-into-the-camera look, demonstratively strike my sunburst Telecaster then tip my head back with my mouth slightly open. Holy shit I must have had that one in me since I was 13, 'cos when I see it back, it ain't bad. Oh look, the whole thing is glorious. Like Bowie and Ronson in '72, Bolan pansying it up with 'Ride a White Swan', Slade performing 'Cum On Feel the Noize' in '73, Gary Glitter (yes, really), the Sweet, Buzzcocks, the Ruts, in fact every band who should never have appeared on *TOTP* but when they did added a frisson of possibility to the drip-dry mainstream. The truth is that after Black Box Recorder's seminal *TOTP* performance of April 2000 at least one person's life will have changed for ever. Such is the power of 'the Pops'. We make it to the end of the song and the cameras drift away and consolidate for the next turn. The audience are once again herded off to the next stage. They're having a good time, this lot, against the odds still smiling as orders are barked at them by some BBC floor manager. A couple of kids remain at the stage as we pack our gear up.

'Excuse me, who are you?' a teen politely enquires as I prepare to make towards my grotty dressing room. *Times have changed*, I think to myself, as I delicately tell the kid who 'we are'.

'Oh,' says a slightly disappointed pop fan. 'Aren't you a bit old for all this?'

With that lethal blow the teen ambles off to watch Usher. Pop music, it's wasted on the young.[19]

[19] Earl Brutus were a chaotic, raucous glam situationist mid-90s rock 'n' roll group fronted by the late, great Nick Sanderson. Brutus had form: Sanderson played in the Gun Club and was another Mary Chain drummer. No spring chickens, this lot. The legend 'Pop Music Is Wasted on the Young' appeared on an Earl Brutus T-shirt.

9

Heaviness going down

May 2000. Go-Betweens revisited and the death of the music industry.

Post Everything: Billionth living person born in India. In London, the nation hangs its head in shame when Tate Modern opens.

In the Post Everything rock 'n' roll world even the Go-Betweens have reformed for the new century. A few weeks after 'The Facts of Life' hits the charts, the greatest pop group since the Monkees – Brisbane's finest, the rekindled Go-Bs – play in London. At the after-show, in amongst the cunts of the backstage free bar, I'm nervous as hell. It's been over ten years since I last spoke to Grant McLennan or Robert Forster. Back then I was a mere tot; a lot has happened. I'm also slightly self-conscious about the fact that some of the early Auteurs songs sailed a bit close – sometimes to the point of mid-sea collision – to the jolly ship

Go-Betweens, particularly under Robert Forster's watch. I'm also aware that this has not gone unnoticed by the big man. Grant McLennan spots me first and throws his arms around me. Full of ebullience, and full of praise for Black Box Recorder. Grant congratulates me on the bona fide hit status of 'The Facts of Life' and buys a bottle of champagne to toast our success. Full of good stuff. Then Robert appears, out of a puff of smoke. Eyebrows arched as ever. Bobby Forster spies me and makes a bee-line.

Before we meditate on how a hit single can immeasurably improve your life, we should take a little time out to ponder the real outcome of Black Box Recorder's brief but palpable dance with the top 20 devil: the irrefutable death of the music industry. Really, no shit. You have of course gathered that this is a highly subjective book, but April 2000 is as convenient a time for me to write an epitaph for the seemingly unfucked yet living and breathing music biz beast as any. Besides, if you want a slightly more measured approach I'm sure you can turn your gaze to one of those faux academic treatises that actually use the great moments in free-thinking music revolution to justify the shamefully lame prose of the majority of music writing. A dastardly Trojan horse and a damn cheek to boot. But remember as you grapple pointlessly with those mirthless pages that none of that mob of ageing ex-music journo fuckers have ever even seen a major label contract, been at the business end of a tour bus, or set foot in a recording studio. Who killed Bambi? I'll tell ya sucker, so listen good.

Day in day out day in day out, sang St Ian Curtis presciently on a track called 'Digital' way back in the dark ages of analogue (1978). And digital is the motherfucker that slowly with a thousand paper cuts put poor old Bambi to death. BBR's *Facts of Life* album is the last elpee that I am involved in that is recorded partially in the analogue mode. The analogue process involves recording audio signal onto magnetic tape. Analogue magnetic tape is, from the second half of the twentieth century to the 1990s, the standard cipher for documenting recorded sound before it is transferred to vinyl (and later CD). The dominance of magnetic tape is no accident, it is the result of extensive scientific audio research into sonic fidelity over the course of many years. In short, the right combination of recorded sound preserved onto tape and then mastered to vinyl sounds fucking great. Damn straight.

The digital recording genocide began in the mid-80s. The old guard – Neil Young is one such detractor – croak and bleat about it being the death of all that is sacred and the hipsters laugh at the moaning old hippies – *Sure, they said the same thing about old pound notes* – but this time, the old guard are right, and the hipsters, with bone-crushing inevitability, just go right ahead and chase the money, as Sony et al latch on to the digital revolution. By the early 90s there is a new buzzword in recording studio technology: Pro Tools. Nirvana's *Nevermind* (1991) is one of the first *big* albums to be recorded using Pro Tools. PT's initial success is down to its editing facilities. Every great record is only as good as its edits, and almost every great record ever made, however 'live' it claims to be, has got a couple of or several hundred edit sections. In analogue, editing is a potentially tricky business, involving skilful one-shot-only splicing together of pieces of tape. Analogue editing is righteously destructive. *Just take a fucking gamble, Campbell.* Pro Tools, on the other hand, allows for infinite non-destructive, non-righteous editing at the click of a mouse. And if you can cut through all that bullshit about the 'infinite possibilities of cut and paste unlimited multitracking', then you might just get down to the real appeal of Pro Tools (digital) recording: it's dirt cheap. By the early twentieth century every cell-of-one-man-band can afford a Pro Tools set-up (or similar: Logic, GarageBand) and can knock out studio-quality toons directly from their laptop and straight into the pop charts. Now that is surely the holy legacy of punk rock? Not quite, sunshine, not quite.

Get with the process you bitter old cunt, warbles the Greek songbird over my shoulder. *Next thing you'll be telling us is that it all sounds the same and you cannot hear the words. Well, let me tell you something for nothing, buster – the parade has passed you by and your chips have well and truly been pissed upon.* Well, perhaps, but it does all sound the same, and that ain't just because I saw the Clash (more of whom later) when I was a wee kiddie. As Pro Tools quickly became an industry (and bedroom) standard, the big old recording studio started to feel like the deserted whorehouse on the edge of the ghost town. What with all those groovy plug-ins that came with that compact Pro Tools set-up, who needed the wailing walls of the ancient recording studio? Elvis, Chuck, Jerry

Lee, that's who. I can feel that I'm losing you. Let me put this another way.

Psycho-acoustics: the sound of leather on willow. When Sam Phillips plugged an RCA valve microphone into an Ampex two-track recorder in July 1954, he wasn't just recording the King's voice, he was recording the King's psyche as he alchemised a harmless old ballad like 'Blue Moon of Kentucky' into what he called 'a pop song'. He was recording the King's Tennessee sweat lingering on the acoustic tiles, he was capturing – on two-track magnetic tape – the scent of every teenage girl the King had finger-fucked back in Tupelo. For ever. When Jerry Lee Lewis sauntered into Sun Studios some two and a half years later, to thrash through 'Whole Lotta Shakin' Goin On', only the devil alone would know for sure just what other psycho-acoustics had been recorded. As 'Strait' James Williamson throttles the treble of his Les Paul on *that* killer riff at the start of 'Search and Destroy', it's not just the sound of an amplifier opening up and bleeding to death: if you listen very carefully you can make out the sound of Iggy's *idiot savant* silver flares – y'know, the ones he's wearing on the back cover of *Raw Power* – flappin' in the breeze. Psycho – acoustics. When you hit 'record' in Pro Tools it's the equivalent of letting a rare butterfly slip through the net. The King's sweat, the finger-fucked teenage girls, Iggy's flares – all converted into binary codes. Never captured, just facsimiled. The aural equivalent of budget-range fish fingers for twenty-first-century ears. If Elvis had been recorded digitally we would have forgotten about him before he'd even joined the army.

Forster's still got it. I'm kind of hoping that like most of the world's population Robert has never heard 'Government Bookstore', an old Auteurs b-side from a time when my *Stop, you've just rewritten a Go-Betweens song* filter was most definitely on the blink. But Robert's like me, nothing escapes him. There is no song too obscure. He's yards away from me now.

'Luke, 's good to see you. How are you?'

Before I can answer he's on to the important business.

'You've just done *Top of the Pops*.' Forster stares at me with some intensity, then as if marvelling at the huge import of what he has just said, lets out a long 'Wooow'. There is a silence: we both understand the heaviness going down.

'What . . . was it like?' says Robert Forster, a man in his mid-forties, eyes wide and full of wonder at the mythological nirvana that is *Top of the Pops*. A true legend.

10

Sam the Bad Cat

May–June 2000. How a hit record will improve your life immeasurably.
Post Everything. Doris Hare, who plays Stan Butler's mother Mabel in 70s TV sitcom On the Buses *dies at the end of May. On 29 June, nine people are killed and 26 injured at a Pearl Jam gig at Roskilde Festival, Denmark. Quick check-up: Primal Scream are still going strong.*

I'm a cat man. If you've read this far then you've probably worked that out. If you have read my first book, *Bad Vibes: Britpop and My Part in Its Downfall* – and let's face it if you are reading this then you probably have – then you will no doubt remember Sam the Bad Cat, Clive Solomon's quisling feline accomplice. Now Sam and I started off on the wrong paw, that's for sure, but never let it be said that a kitty cannot change its claws once in one of its lifetimes. Since the dark days of '92 Sam and I have stayed – intermittently – in touch, at first exchanging occasional letters and then with the advancement of technology through the wretched email. Now, in the late spring of 2000, old Sam has turned up at the big dilapidated house in Tufnell Park looking a bit the worse for wear. I am of course pleased to see my four-footed friend but I can tell something is wrong. We exchange how dos and pleasantries only as a cat and a man who have not seen each other for a while can, then it is down to business.

'What's the real story, Sam?' I enquire of the drunken moggie.

'Got into a bit of trouble on the subcontinent,' slurs Sam.

'India?' I say.

'That area,' answers Sam, shifting from unsteady paw to unsteady paw. 'Got a job as a ratter with a hermetic sect just outside of Rangoon. Heard too much – the mysteries of the East, all that malarkey . . .'

'The O.T.O.?' ask I, nervously. Old four paws' eyes dart from left to right. Silence. Then Sam the Bad Cat briefly reverts to animal language, letting out a huge drunken meow. 'All right, I admit it, I got confused,' babbles the furry fiend. 'I was falling into typical ignorant-Westerner behaviour, mistaking unfamiliar customs and practices as acts of menace. I'm no racist though. It was a classic school-cat error.'

'For Christ's sake, Sam, put a lid on it, sunshine,' I say to the addled pussy. 'Look, you can stay here for a week, in the attic with the dirty pigeons, but you must be discreet. My wife-to-be cannot know that I keep counsel with a talking cat.'

'You're a life saver, pal,' says Sam, the booze starting to make him sentimental. I lean down and pick him up.

'Come on, I'll give you a hand up to the attic.'

'What's been happening in my absence then?' asks the cat as we ascend several flights of stairs.

'Not a lot, but Pulp did all right.'

'Jesus,' says Sam the drunk Bad Cat.

Sam's been settling in well. On evenings when I have nothing better to do I join him after he has had his evening meal; we shoot the breeze over a blissful opium pipe or whatever narcotics Sam is willing to share from his travels in the Orient. I am crouched by the water tank when the cat jumps down beside me, feathers from a filthy poisoned pigeon carcass still stuck to his mouth and teeth.

'That's disgusting,' I say.

'Fuck off, I'm a cat,' says the cat not unreasonably.

'Do you fancy some laudanum? It was given to me as a pre-wedding gift.' I offer the phial to the cat, who manages to lick a couple of drops of the highly hallucinogenic opiate from his dirty claw.

'I just can't work out my next move after being on *Top of the Pops*. John and Sarah loved that shit, but I just feel kind of embarrassed. I'm hanging out with writers, playwrights and film makers – I have ideas above my station,' I continue.

'You're just too, too coooool for schooool,' drawls the slightly stoned cat, adding somewhat unnecessarily, 'and I'm a real coool kitty too.'

'I was gonna make a bizarre hip-hop album with Mos Def

but Biggie Smalls told me it was a terrible idea.' I am suddenly aware of how ridiculous this sentence sounds as I say it out loud, but Sam's fur remains unruffled.

'Don't worry about it, I'm a talking cat, nothing surprises me. I do like Notorious B.I.G. 'Mo Money Mo Problems' is my favourite. Do you think you could introduce me?'

'No,' I shoot back, 'besides, Smalls is long dead and I have no idea when he's going to commune with me next. Anyway, I thought the only band you liked was the Blue Aeroplanes?'

'Biggie Smalls is dead? Jeez,' says Sam. 'When, how, why?'

'The east coast, west coast rap wars. Tupac's dead as well,' I add, filling in the cat on some recent rap history.

'Strewth,' says Sam, jumping up on top of the water tank, deliberately swishing me with his tail on the way.

'Look, can we get back to the subject? You're the one who knows the mysteries of the east – you tell me what to do,' I sneer up at the mardy cat.

'OK,' says Sam. 'But first you have an apology to make.'

'I'm listening.' I think Sam the Bad Cat is about to get holier than thou on my ass.

'You should try and make it up to Saul Galpern. He's not a bad man. I mean I know I'm a cat an' all, and the rivalries between the old firms must be respected, but all that business with Marnie the tiny dog . . . well, it was just . . . retarded.'

'Thank you, Sam,' I sulk back, chastened somewhat. 'I'll apologise, but what I really need to know is what should I do next?' Sam scratches his ear with his paw and has a think.

The only sounds are the slow drip of the water tank and a distant tap of Siân typing in the room below.

'Have you heard of Nicholas van Hoogstraten, the dandyish property developer, who's pals with Robert Mugabe and refers to his rental tenants as scum?' asks the cat.

'You mean the guy who's building a fake pharaoh's palace for himself on the South Downs?' I counter.

'Yep, the very same one,' says Sam. 'Well, write a stage musical about him. Now, can you tell me all about the east coast, west coast rap wars?'

'Some other time,' I say. Sam the Bad Cat hisses at me in a disappointed manner before jumping behind the water tank, looking for more dead pigeons.

John and Sarah are having a party to coincide with the transmission on Friday evening of Black Box Recorder's inaugural appearance on *Top of the Pops*.[20] I don't bother going. Siân and I go to the pub on our own instead. I've had enough of all this self-celebration. The record company wants to repeat the hit single feat with our next offering, 'The Art of Driving', thus perpetuating the never-ending vicious circle

[20] *Top of the Pops* changes its transmission time from Thursday to Friday in 1996, in a series of many attempts to revamp what the BBC considers to be an ageing format. All this really achieves is the loss of the 'talk about it in the school playground factor the morning after' that the original Thursday time slot effortlessly had. A broadsheet journalist snidely writes that after BBR's appearance on *TOTP* our record slips down the charts. Not so. The show is recorded on Tuesday, when, as is often the case, the single had already descended several places from its top 20 peak.

of hit single, hit album, ad infinitum or until madness or death take their toll. I feel like an old gangster who's just pulled off a successful heist. For some the temptation to go back and pull off one last caper is strong, but not I. Fuck it, let's just be a one-hit wonder band – better than a no-hit wonder band. It's the simpering that gets to me, and to be in the pop rat race you have to leave your brain at the door and simper. *Would you just do a couple of radio station 'idents'?*

'Hi, I'm Luke Haines from Black Box Recorder and you're listening to radio D.U.M.B. FM.'

We've got you a spot on The Big Breakfast, *we'll send a car to pick you up at 5 a.m. Yeah, I know that's the morning after your Radio 1 evening session, but it's a really important promo slot for us, they still get a lot of viewers you know. No, it's OK, Chris Evans doesn't do that show any more. We've booked you on a 9 a.m. flight to Cologne, that's all that was available, you should be able to make it on time as long as you leave the TV studio straight after your interview. Oh, by the way, the* Big Breakfast *producers have asked if you mind being interviewed by some puppets – after they've performed a cover of your song on kazoo. One last thing, bring a change of clothing with you, it's a pretty anarchic show. Good fun though, everyone who's been on it has said what a laugh it is.*

You can never win the pop rat race. So, at 32 years of age I decide I am too old, too much of a smart arse, and, oddly, too sane for this kind of caper. I deselect myself. In May, Siân and I get married. I still love proper pop – as an observer. Now, about that musical based upon the life of Nicholas van Hoogstraten . . .

11

Piss and mustard

July–August 2000. Black Box Recorder go forth and go camp, and have a (semi-) hit album.

Post Everything. On 25 July an Air France Concorde crashes minutes after take-off from Roissy Charles de Gaulle Airport. All 109 passengers are killed. Channel 4 shows the first series of rum Dutch-originated social cohesion drill Big Brother. *In rock, normal service is resumed when Black Box Recorder's second single from* The Facts of Life *album, 'The Art of Driving', achieves a chart position of number 58. Pulp and Oasis headline Reading and Leeds festivals.*

Of course, I do not get the chance to deselect myself. I mean, as if. Oh no, the Great British Public will see to any clever-clever plans that I have up my sleeve. My noble gesture of walking away from my career as a hitmaker has gone unacknowledged. You see, it's all a question of timing. Perhaps it would have been better to announce that I am opting out of having hit singles just *before* having one. Maybe I should have worn a T-shirt on *Top of the Pops* saying, 'This is the last time you will see me on this programme – I'm off, back to the distant perimeter of rock', but I didn't do that, I just went through the motions, miming away like the thousands of cretins who came before me. Opting out of a career as a hitmaker before having a flop single is less convincing. The writing is on the wall. First, the *Facts of Life* album goes in the album charts, in the thirties, weirdly lower than expected, confirming everyone's great fear (but mine) that we have just had a novelty hit, i.e. the kids who bought the single just ain't interested in buying the album. Then, the follow-up single, 'The Art of Driving' (a so-near-the-knuckle-it's-halfway-up-the-elbow duet), featuring Moore and Nixey cooing how's ya father euphemisms at one another (am I missing something?), tries to duck under the VIP cordon of the top 40, only to be led away by security. None of which really matters. The music industry is amazed that I have been allowed into the singles chart. Saul Galpern and I manage to make up, with the Scotsman even agreeing to a new BBR album. I allow myself a smile, thinking about the Marnie Dog. Boy, did calling that mutt a cunt ever pay off. I even manage to keep shtum about my plans to be marginal, as Saul mentions a substantial advance. For one short summer in 2000, with one modest hit single and one even more modest hit album above the door, Black Box Recorder still manage to go imperial.

2000. Year of the charts. A year in which Black Box

Recorder consolidate their almost weapons-grade success by doing three gigs. Three gigs. Hahahaha. Unfortunately, Black Box Recorder are a band with some degree of democracy – John and I get an even share on the songwriting and Sarah has the (tacit) power of veto. We are that most useless of things: a committee. Ideas are put forward: *Shall we go on tour?* Of course, someone (usually me) doesn't want to. *How about getting 500 promotional frisbees made up and giving them away with the new single?*[21] *By the way what is the new single? Oh, we can't agree. Never mind, we'll think about it next week. Shall we go to the pub?* Deadlines come and go, any momentum gained is soon lost. Black Box Recorder, as an operation, is a bit of a shambles. So the first public performance of our mammoth live triathlon takes place at London's tiny Colony Room club in Soho, in front of an audience of maybe 30. The Colony is perhaps BBR's natural habitat, where old Soho ('. . . I'm in imports and exports, old chap, at least that's what I tell the boys in blue') rubs up against the obnoxious and dim new art bores ('We're vegetarians and we're just really *really* into the Sex Pistols, have you heard of the Situationists?'). It's a blast, albeit a fleeting one for we are a pro act now, and we have a couple of dates with that most heinous of modern institutions: the English Summer Music Festival.

*

[21] The finest example of democracy at work? A Black Box Recorder promotional mug with Lord Lucan's face and the legend 'National Disgrace'. No band name appears.

August bank holiday weekend. Reading Festival, backstage bar. As any pensionable old music biz whore will tell you, the Reading Festival backstage bar is a heathen hellhole, and it is here on a late-summer Friday night that I am not so much holding court as being held up après BBR's third and final gig of the year. With questionable logic Black Box Recorder have accepted an offer to play the festival sandwiched between new hard rock favourites Queens of the Stone Age and older hard rock favourites Nashville Pussy. If you are unfamiliar with the Pussy, I'll make it easy: they sound very much like how you would expect a band from Texas called Nashville Pussy to sound. That said, our hard rock spit roasting shouldn't be too much of a problem. We are on top of our game and our self-belief is cast iron. An unsuitable billing would normally be a trifling irritation but for one small matter: as the advance for the new album has yet to materialise the BBR coffers are empty. So we take the expedient measure of dispensing with our rock-solid rhythm section and spend our performance fee on hiring two pilot's uniforms for Moore and myself. This, of course, does not pass without incident – when John Moore realises that he has one less stripe on the sleeve of his jacket than me, a seamstress is quickly despatched to sew on the 'missing' stripe. With Nixey kitted out as an air stewardess, we are ready to er, rock Reading. We ascend the ramp onto the stage, with more than a little trepidation. Three overly and unintentionally camp idiots armed with only a guitar, a saw, and some sarcasm – just what nobody really wants after the festival-friendly bludgeoning of the Queens of the Stone Age.

'Good evening, we're Black Box Recorder,' says Sarah to an indifferent crowd. 'We'll be cruising at an altitude of approximately fifteen feet, we hope you have a pleasant flight.' *Jesus Christ*, I think to myself, trying not to knock off my ridiculous pilot's hat as I strap on my guitar. *I'm about to find out what it feels like to be fucked hard up the ass.*

Having completed our grizzly turn, we head down the ramp that takes us off stage. We stood our ground and I am still able to walk. John gallantly escorts Sarah by delicately taking her hand. *What is going on?* Our show wasn't so bad, but that's the thing about festivals, they are the great hom-ogeniser of music. No one is good, no one is bad, even the artists don't know what kind of performance they've just turned in, the only thing that matters is not running over your allotted playing time. It's all about piss and mustard: the ability to pass muster, no more, no less. I walk through the real punters until I get to the relative safety of the backstage bar, where instead of congratulating us on our performance people say things like 'Well, you survived *that*.' I decide to go back to the anonymity of the punter bar area, where Moore and I, now hitting our post-gig drunken stride – and still dressed as pilots – spend the rest of the evening doing our best to terrify gullible youngsters on drugs.

Gullible Youngster on Drugs: 'So is there an airfield nearby?'

Me. 'Nope, we put her down in Stanstead this afternoon, then caught the train up. We'll catch a few bands before flying on the redeye tonight over to JFK,' I say, beckoning to Moore, who has somehow procured a pint of vodka and tonic, which he thrusts into my hand, the hand that is not preoccupied with a half-empty bottle of wine and a hip flask.

'You mean you're going to fly . . . tonight?' says the youngster.

'Of course we're going to fucking fly, we are pilots. We fly,' roars Moore.

'Just a few straightener-outers to steady the nerves,' I add.

'None of us pilots like to be too sober before take-off,' butts in a wobbly Moore, pushing it somewhat, 'nothing a few lines of coke won't sort out.'

The Gullible Young Person on Drugs stares at the two pissed pilots before him. He has made a vow to himself that he will never fly again. Feeling that we have done some good and are merely spreading a little happiness, Moore and I replay our dubious act a few more times to a few more lucky campers, to the point where even we start to believe our own bullshit.

I awake too early in a hotel bed still dressed as a fucking pilot. We are to rendezvous with the rest of our party – John Moore, Sarah Nixey, Manager Charlie, a PR who keeps on poking a film camera in my face, and a couple of our road crew – to take our unintentionally camp[22] act up the

[22] As acts go 'Hard Poof' is OK, but requires consummate skill, and in the early stages can prove very tricky to pull off. 'Camp' can often fall between two stools, but 'Unintentionally Camp' is unforgivable.

motorway to Leeds,[23] to complete the final part of our festival double header. Boy, are those northerners gonna love us. Not being any kind of fan of groups – especially ones that I am in – and not being any kind of team player my natural disposition is to encourage dysfunction; Siân and I have achieved this by travelling separately from the main party in our tiny sports car. We meet the tour bus only at the service station and bid each other a safe journey, before whizzing off with the top down, leaving only a trail of dust and a lumbering tour bus with its slightly miffed contents. The last laugh of course always belongs to someone else. There is no more stupid sight than a man in an open-top sports car on his way to Leeds dressed as a fucking pilot. *Those two*, I think to myself as we hurtle up the M1 feeling every fucking lump in the road, *they're behaving in a really familiar way with each other. Surely not, they wouldn't be so . . . surely not. They're not, they can't be.*

[23] In the late twentieth century/early twenty-first century, organisers of the Reading Festival decide to rinse a little more money out of the fest-happy public: bands playing at the Reading Festival are now required to play an extra show in Leeds. This proves to be a miserable experience for both audience and performers. Tired bands give half-hearted performances in a half-empty northern field on a depressing August bank holiday Monday.

12

They are

September 2000. In which we find out what exactly is going on with The Other Two.
Post Everything. UK fuel protests: lorry drivers and farmers blockade oil facilities in protest against rising petrol prices. On 30 September the Maze Prison in Northern Ireland – of H Blocks and Bobby Sands notoriety – is closed.

Surely not . . . They can't be . . . Can they?

Oh. They are.

13

Theorem of the moron

October 2000. And the eternal question is: should the fucking band really be exchanging fluids with one another? Plus, the strange and true story of the pre-unification Beatles Deniers of West Germany.
Post Everything. Second Intifada in Israel. On 17 October four people are killed and 70 are injured in the Hatfield rail crash. Sony PlayStation 2 released.

If you are ever unlucky or lucky enough to find yourself in a rock band, and you achieve a modicum of success – i.e. when you know you are talking shit yet no one will take you to task on the matter – it will soon become apparent that there are ample opportunities to behave like a total moron. You are a kid in the proverbial candy shop, or perhaps, more accurately, a fucktard in the adult literary centre. In rock 'n' roll, cretinous behaviour is exalted:

drive the wrong way up the freeway (Ace Frehley out of Kiss); drive the wrong way up the freeway with one hand on your crystal meth pipe whilst packing a revolver (David Crosby[24]); develop a gargantuan cocaine habit and insist upon bragging about your Vietnam war record in front of your own road crew, who are all painfully aware that you were having hits with the Buffalo Springfield at the time of the Vietnam war (Stephen Stills). Or, if it's simplicity you're after, you could try being carried upside down by your legs and then dropped on your head – breaking your neck in the process, like the drummer from Motörhead (Filthy Phil 'Animal' Taylor). But for sheer poetic beauty you could achieve the holy grail of idiocy as Brian Harvey out of E17 once did, by eating a burger so quickly that you are sick, then getting in your car, reversing, and somehow running yourself over in the process, ending a glorious evening in intensive care. All of the preceding will be permitted. But even in a trade as nebulous as showbiz there is still one golden 'don't' that should never be breached, a big fat line that must never be crossed: the intra-band relationship.

In 1981, Professor Karl Wilkie of the Leipzig Institute of Cranial Research published his first academic paper, *Das Theorem vom Trottel* ('The Theorem of the Moron') revealing the results of eight years' extensive research into rock music and its relationship to the lower IQ. After the presentation,

[24] 'I got arrested for something I didn't do,' quoth the Cros, 'I didn't hide the drugs and I didn't hide the guns.'

the Institute's trust fund was appalled at Professor Wilkie's findings, and in a controversy that rocked German academia to its foundations, Wilkie's studies were immediately terminated, resulting in the professor being expelled from the Leipzig Institute. Wilkie's associates were stinging in their criticism of their colleague: '*Es gibt nur einen Trottel im Zimmer und das ist Karl Wilkie*' ('There is only one moron in the room and that is Karl Wilkie'), said Dr Günter Schröder. Pastor Wilhelm Aust of the Munster Christian Brothers was even more damning: '*Der Mann ist ein friggin' Zeit Waster.*' On becoming a pariah a lesser man would have been crushed, but not Wilkie. In 1985 the former academic was to be found in the UK, falsely claiming unemployment benefits and living in Nuneaton. The devil had been making plenty of work for Wilkie's idle hands, and by the end of the year what was once a mere 20,000 word academic paper had grown into a monstrous tome. *Theorem of the Moron* by Professor Karl. H. Wilkie was published in 1986 to a fanfare of indifference. Wilkie had of course been driven insane by almost a decade of extensive research, and at the end of the year was sectioned under the Mental Health Act. By the end of the 80s the professor, a cross-dresser since his early teens, had undergone a sex change operation and changed his name to Carol. Carol was last heard of running a caravan site in Leigh-on-Sea, Essex.

Wilkie's book over the years has become something of a sacred text, spoken of in hushed tones by many a scholar of rock. A pox upon any music journalist who hasn't tried to tackle at least two chapters of Wilkie's terrible prose. As well as musing on the optimum IQ of a rock star (83, though Wilkie puts forward a compelling argument over the course of seven chapters in favour of mild mental retardation) and the correct height for pop (4 feet 11 inches for females, 5 feet 4 inches for men), and issuing a maverick statement on the advantages of male pattern baldness in middle-aged rock 'n' rollers, the author contends that, all things considered, it is better not to be able to havc the same haircut that you had at 18 when you are 52. (It is fair to assume that Paul Weller is one of many who have not read the work of Karl Wilkie.) One of *Theorem of the Moron*'s (*TOTM*) more outré claims is that the drummer is not the biggest moron in any given rock group. The biggest moron, according to Wilkie, is in fact the lead singer or the 'front man'. Interestingly, the professor asserts that with the exception of Chrissie Hynde, women are exempt from *TOTM*. It is thought that at the time of writing these most controversial chapters of the book, the professor had already begun his journey towards becoming 'Carol'. Wilkie expands his thesis further, claiming that there are two strands of moron: moron positive and moron negative. As examples Wilkie cites Ozzy Osbourne as M-positive and the lead singer out of U2 as M-negative.[25] Indeed, it is

[25] Other examples of 'M-positive': the first four Kiss albums; Status Quo – shockingly up to and including 'Whatever You Want'; and the short career of Dee Dee Ramone as a rapper. For M-negative: Oasis (included more for their dull-brained fans than the dull-brained group); Mötley Crüe; all Kiss members' solo albums; and all of Ozzy's post-Sabbath activities.

perhaps useful to cite Sabbath's classic Vertigo period as the prime example of what the professor describes in chapters 42–47 as *The hierarchy of the moron.*[26] Regarding M-negative, or, simply put, *bad moronic*, the author succinctly writes that 'a detailed career study of U2 is in no way cost-effective'. In German, obviously.

So what does the good doctor have to say of the 'intra-band relationship'? Well, he's dead against it, as you might imagine. '*Verboten!*' as he succinctly puts it in chapter 51. Indeed, parts of TOTM pertaining to this question are without doubt the book's most controversial – and some would say downright sacrilegious – passages. Karl Wilkie

[26] Over the course of six albums between 1970 and 1975 Black Sabbath created some of the dumbest, slowest, knuckle-dragging rock music previously unheard, pre-empting or inventing, however you want to think about it, such dum-dum sub-genres as heavy metal and stoner rock. Over the course of the first three albums (*Black Sabbath*, *Paranoid*, and *Master of Reality*) Tony Iommi pounds out brain-dribbling gonzo riffs only to have lead singer Ozzy Osbourne howl back the melody complete with some of the stupidest lyrics – mainly written by bass player Terry 'Geezer' Butler – ever committed to half-inch high-oxide magnetic tape. Ozzy sings like a man on a mission to find the missing part of his brain. By 1975's *Sabotage*, their most psychologically damaged record (just look at the sleeve), it is clear that the mission to find Ozzy's brain will have to be aborted. Somehow these albums transcend all of the aforementioned and creep into the subconscious like a crafty cat burglar. When asked about the making of these albums, drummer Bill Ward speaks of a 'fifth' member of the band, an unseen occult presence guiding the group. Armed with this fantastic knowledge listeners can only submit themselves wholly to the Sab's scorched-earth reality trip. Without doubt some of the greatest rock 'n' roll ever made. These records fucking swing, man.

was a Beatles Denier, one of a shadowy group of people in pre-unification West Germany who refused to believe in the face of overwhelming evidence that so-called Beatle-mania ever happened, and that the amount of people who bought Beatles records was vastly exaggerated. (Wilkie estimates that as of 1986 *Sgt Pepper's Lonely Hearts Club Band* had sold 'fewer than 70 copies'.) Since 1990, Beatles Denying has been outlawed by the European Parliament and *Mojo* magazine, and since this law was passed copies of *TOTM* have had one specific chapter edited out. '*Ach nein, das Wife's auf Tastaturen*' ('Oh no, the wife's on keyboards') deals most explicitly with Wilkie's Beatles Denial and also makes a compelling case in favour of Yoko Ono, claiming that Lennon's post-Beatles career was improved immeasurably by his Japanese wife sitting next to him on stage wearing a blindfold, as he performed 'Instant Karma' on *Top of the Pops*. Maybe it's time to put *Theorem of the Moron* down for a while. I'm sure we will return to it later on.

After BBR's exhausting commitment to live appearances in support of the *Facts of Life* album has been completed (now reaching a heady total of five gigs), I return to the studio in September 2000, to begin work on my first solo album 'proper'. On a dull Tuesday afternoon my mobile phone rings. I don't like these things – these travel blowers – I haven't worked out how to turn the fucker off and I don't like being contactable at any time of the fucking day. It's John Moore. I haven't heard from John for a few weeks – I've been busy being married, writing songs and taking advice from talking cats. Turns out that John Moore has been doing his own thing too.

'I've been meaning to tell you for some time but the time is never right,' begins Old Moore down the other end of the dog and bone. This is an ominous start to a conversation. 'It's about Sarah and me . . .' Aha, it would seem that the love that dare not speak its name is now daring to speak its name. It's not a surprise. I'm kind of hoping this is just some sort of fling, but I know it isn't. I know that there is no opinion worth sharing when it comes to people and people they like sharing bodily fluids with. All I will say is, I have form with the intra-band relationship. It ain't good. There are many rock 'n' roll clichés – here's another: being in a band is like being in a marriage. If this is true, does this mean that BBR will have a marriage within a marriage? Could anyone possibly believe that sounds promising? It's the beginning of the end. Whatever kind of juju we cooked up to write the first two albums will have changed, as will the intra-band 'politics'. Put simply, Black Box Recorder just won't be as good. I tell John that I'm pleased for him and Sarah before ringing off. We are both relieved to end the conversation. I put the new 'intra-band relationship' to the back of my mind and get back to work in the studio.

14

'This is Dr Strange, I'll put you on hold, I've got the Angel of Death on the other line'

November 2000–January 2001. A 'high-art-hip-hop-pastiche concept album' that the record company people do not like very much – until they change their minds. Elsewhere, a run-in with the Compte de Saint-Germain, and for those who are interested a digested cut-out-and-keep guide to the Situationist International. Post Everything. George W. Bush defeats Al Gore in US presidential election, despite disputed votes in the state of Florida. Pop mogul Jonathan King is charged with three child sex offences dating back 32 years, and relating to boys that he picked up at the Walton Hop, a disco in Walton-on-Thames, Surrey, my place of birth. A criminal gang make a botched attempt to steal the De Beers Millennium Star diamond from the Millennium Dome. By the end of the year the Dome has closed. In January 2001, Wikipedia goes online, and the first series of global 'brand' Pop Stars *is shown on ITV.*

Christmas 2000, Manager Charlie and I sit in the plush offices of Hut Records. The label is getting more and more successful, more and more people are being employed and more expensive office tat is being bought, and last and always least – more rubbish groups are being signed. MC and I are here to give The Boyd the exclusive on my new album, *The Oliver Twist Manifesto*. I still like DB, he leaves me alone to record and lets me do what I want. He's regretting that now. You see, David Boyd is not digging my new album. Dave always digs my new albums, sometimes with a few minor caveats, but this is different. This could be very bad. Album playbacks are always excruciatingly painful experiences for all parties. If you're an A & R man every tick, click, and sigh will be scrutinised by the beady, greedy – *please like me* – little eyes of band and manager. You will require the best damn poker face in the business and masterful control of your own body language to get through the album playback. Dave's just about got the poker face thing covered but his body language is fucked – he really couldn't be retreating into himself much more as he hides behind his big boss man desk.

'Have you got any spliff?' says The Boyd, in need of some relaxation.

'Nah, I don't smoke any more,' I say, opening up a conversational B-road that will allow DB and me to awkwardly chew over the pros and cons of 'not smoking any more', whilst something that to the untrained ear may sound like an odd sort of hip-hop pastiche thunders out of the enormous record company speakers. Right on cue Boyd's bodily retreat begins tout de suite towards the end of the first line of the first track, 'Rock and Roll Communique Number One', as I grimly warble the lyric, 'This is not entertainment . . .' By track two, *Oliver Twist*, a splenetic pro-imagination tirade, with a slow broken Dr Dre backbeat, I watch as the A & R man's facial expression settles into a rictus grimace. By the third number, something called 'The Death of Sarah Lucas', I can tell that I've lost DB. Perhaps this is to be expected. Hut Records' most recent activities have included putting out a piss poor 'Look, ma, I'm a grown-up singer-songwriter' album by the singer out of The Verve, and signing a group called the Music, a bunch of Northerners who sound like a mini-pops The Verve. It should be of no surprise that El Davo is giving my comedy rants about brain-ache Brit artists short shrift, but it has kind of caught me off guard. I feel I am wandering into unfamiliar territory – the A & R guy has never pulled this one on me before. Even when I was offering up proto versions of the *How I Learned to Love the Bootboys* album there were criticisms, but fundamentally Dave was with me. Now, well, if the atmosphere gets much colder then things are gonna turn hostile. The big man snaps when we get midway through the fourth song, a homage to the Situationist International called 'Never Work'[27] in the

[27] The Situationist International (SI) deliberately set out to be difficult to define: a group of artists and writers who were against art. Avant-garde provocateurs who opposed both provocation and the avant-garde. War-gaming nihilists and revolutionary agitators. The Situationists were one helluva chippy crew. Established in 1957, and 'led' ruthlessly and egotistically by Guy Debord. In the first issue of *Internationale Situationniste* – the group's peerless periodical, published between 1958 and 1969, the term

style of T. Rex's 'Ballrooms of Mars'. The Boyd looks up grumpily during the 'Ne Travaillez Jamais . . .' section of

---

'Situationist' is defined thus: 'Having to do with the theory or practical activity of constructing situations. One who engages in the construction of situations.' In 1967, Debord's treatise *The Society of the Spectacle* was first published in France. According to Debord's theory, the Spectacle – the state-sponsored consumer society – is all-powerful and capable of recuperating even the most radical situations; the only chance of overcoming the Spectacle is through violent overthrow. Debord's words were prescient; on 3 May 1968, on a sweltering Friday evening, Paris exploded in a maelstrom of rioting. Plenty has been written about May '68, and during those weeks the SI briefly entered the national psyche of La République, as graffiti slogans, 'Never Work', 'Boredom Is Counter Revolutionary', 'Scream, Steal, Ejaculate Your Desires' (authored by Situationist Raoul Vaneigem), appeared around the city. Debord and Co's greatest propaganda coup came on 15 May when along with several other insurrectionary groups (including Maoist, Trotskyist, and violent anarchist factions) they occupied the Sorbonne, brandishing a flag claiming the building in the name of the Comité Enragés-Internationale Situationniste. France's most revered seat of learning was now in the hands of revolutionaries. Debord rode the Paris uprising for all it was worth. By 1972, all SI members apart from Debord had been expelled, but the group's influence had spread to the UK, with Situationist-influenced groups such as King Mob – named in homage to the Gordon Riots – springing up. In 1971 a spate of terrorist bombings by a cell who called themselves the Angry Brigade brought the near defunct SI to the attention of the Home Office. This UK mob's activities were often accompanied by Situationist-style communiqués. Punk year zero, 1976, saw Vaneigem's and Chris Grey's (King Mob and SI member) sloganeering famously co-opted by Malcom McLaren, Bernie Rhodes and Jamie Reid in the sleeve design and anti-marketing strategy of the Sex Pistols, and to a lesser degree the Clash product. John Lydon has never mentioned the Situationists.

the chorus and snaps, 'Not exactly 'Junk Shop Clothes', is it.' I use no words in my response, just an audible sideways sneer out of the top corner of my mouth. Dave's been spending too much time with his stable of northern dunces and my Situationist-referencing Franglais has tickled the bell on his pseudometer.

'What I mean,' says the A & R, with deadly aim, 'is that it lacks your usual élan.' Haha. OK, touché, old chap. Well, what did you fucking expect, hits?

The recordings that become *The Oliver Twist Manifesto* are born out of a strange sense of outsiderdom – stranger than usual at least. After Moore and Nixey's 'announcement' that they are now an item I feel like an outcast in my own group. There is talk from BBR's label (Nude) that we should get to work quickly on the follow-up to *The Facts of Life*. John and Sarah are both keen to follow this course of action. I am not. If I'm going to make a record it's going to be on my own, on my own terms, and it is going to sound nothing like the last Black Box Recorder album. For now, it's back to the cell of one.

I have been 'given' a free slate to do what I want by David Boyd: unlimited budget, unlimited time, unlimited resources. As usual I don't have unlimited material. As usual I have no material. Would I even bother making records if I didn't have all these fucking record contracts? I wonder to myself; perhaps I would just while away my hours in a stupor, talking to cats and very occasionally coming up with the odd ditty, just for my own amusement. My inertia stems partly from the dabbling dilettante phase which I am currently going through and partly from my total utter boredom with the 'task' of songwriting. The turgid, craftsman-like, artisan drudge of chipping away at a song makes me want to scream. David Boyd's words of a few years ago are still with me: 'You're not ready to make your singer-songwriter album yet.' Damn straight, and that's one thing you ain't gonna get.

I have become obsessed with concepts. Two concepts in particular: concept art (mainly useless) and high-concept rap. Over the summer Eminem's latest, *The Marshall Mathers LP*, is rarely out of earshot. Dr Dre too. The video for Em's 'Real Slim Shady' is everywhere – man it's so good it almost makes me want to cry. If I am having some kind of early midlife crisis then I am at least enjoying it. My initial idea for the album is to serve up a kind of avant-garde karaoke: I'll blow the recording budget on paying for the synchronisation rights for a bunch of current hits and I'll just re-release them under my own name – of course, this is a legal minefield and I quickly drop this mental plan. The next idea is to record short disturbing sketches against a blurred ambient backdrop. Unfortunately Chris Morris has had the exact same idea (before me), which he puts to startling effect in his *Blue Jam* television series, with accompanying soundtrack album. Finally, song fragments start coming. Following on from the advice given to me by a dead rapper and a talking cat, I have long since abandoned any plans to be produced by Mos Def, or any of the Rawkus mob, but my interest in Eminem has reawakened something. It is obvious, it must have been staring me in the face for months; what I need to do is make a high-art-hip-hop-pastiche concept album, on my own – no collaboration required. Throw in a few Masonic references and the odd nod to the Paupers' Crusade and we'll have a cat-in-bag-in-river situation. You'll need a guide book to understand this muthafucka.

Recording begins in October 2000 and ends just before Christmas, the job is quick and clean, I have enough studio connections to access and assimilate all the hippest beats. I'm just doing what every white guy has done since the early days of the blues: I'm robbing the black man of his music. The songs are almost entirely recorded in the order they appear on the album. The two versions of the title track, 'Oliver Twist' and 'The Oliver Twist Manifesto', are pretty much copped from Dr Dre's international smash 'Forget About Dre'. Unfortunately the best bit of the lyric – the 'got to pick a pocket or two' line, sung by a children's choir – eventually gets edited out when its author, Lionel Bart, or Lionel Bart's publishers at least, refuse to give copyright permission. 'The Death of Sarah Lucas' is a straightforward assassination fantasy poem over an A minor drone, in which I cast myself as a modern-day Valerie Solanas with Lucas as my Warhol quarry. (Just before the record's release this number gets played to its subject, who rather predictably claims to like it.) 'Mr and Mrs Solanas' continues the art/murder theme against a backdrop of my own recent wedding. 'Discomania', originally recorded as part of the soundtrack to the still unreleased movie *Christie Malry's Own Double-Entry*, gets a workover. Man, we spend a small fortune on this baby, the final touches being the multitracked recorders on the chorus, added as a homage to Eminem's 'Real Slim Shady'. Even amongst this line-up of misfits, perhaps the oddest track on *The Oliver Twist Manifesto* is the final song to be recorded: 'The Spook Manifesto'. One afternoon in a break from studio activity I am sitting in a quiet Camden pub when I notice a man a few tables away having an increasingly voluble and distressing conversation on his mobile phone. Charles Manson/Catweazle lookalike mentalists are not exactly in short supply in the side streets of London NW1, but this spooked nuisance makes my blood run cold. The crazy addresses someone called Lucy, who may or may not be on the other end of the line. He refers to himself as both the Comte de Saint-Germain[28] and Dr Strange. At times the freak breaks off his 'conversation' with 'Lucy' to announce that he has 'the angel of death on the other line'. The mentalist keeps me pinned to my chair with his wild-eyed stare throughout his discourse. I can't shift the incident from my mind until it eventually becomes the entire lyric for 'The Spook Manifesto'. So then, *The Oliver Twist Manifesto*, a cod hip-hop concept album with recorders and a children's choir, featuring songs about crusaders, art murderers, and occultist shape shifters. Cameos from King Mob (see Situationist footnote, p. 100), Michèle Bernstein and Raoul

[28] The Count of Saint-Germain (1710–84), courtier, alchemist, magician, charlatan, crops up in many occult histories and threads. Credited with god-like powers and a century-straddling lifespan. There are individuals who have claimed encounters with Saint-Germain in the twentieth century.

Vaneigem, and just for good measure a few references to the Letterists.[29] Now what the hell do you do with a record like this?

[29] The Letterist Internationale – avant-garde 40s Left Bank existentialists led by Isidore Isou, natural precursors to the Situationist International. The group made headlines worldwide in 1950, when one of their number, Michel Mourre, interrupted an Easter mass at Notre-Dame Cathedral, disguised as a Dominican monk, and read a sermon declaring 'The death of God'.

15

'He's thinking of marketing. I'm not'

April–July 2001. *A big idea, a manifesto, and a state-of-the-nation address.*
Post Everything. John Prescott successfully lamps an egg-throwing farm worker. Silvio Berlusconi wins Italian general election, and four more years New Labouring after 7 June general election in the UK. John Lee Hooker, Jack Lemmon, and Joan Sims all die.

What do we do with a record like this? David Boyd has been pondering this very question. Boyd has been 'living' with what I hope will be my new record over the Christmas period, and over the first few months of 2001. In early April, Manager Charlie and I are summoned to the record company office. We sit in reception with some anxiety waiting to be allowed 'up'. This will be a make-or-break meeting.

It's the former. The Boyd has finally decided that he 'gets' the record; all we have to do now is work out what 'to do' with the damn thing. My initial thought is that maybe 'releasing' it would be a good place to start, this apparently would be too simple.

'How about entering it for the Turner Prize?' I suggest, only half joking. Dave Boyd's eyes light up – oh God, if I'm not careful we could get into another sack of bullshit exchange scenario. As we're all digging each other again, I decide I may as well chance my arm on a bit of outstanding business: the *Christie Malry* soundtrack that was recorded over a year ago is still languishing in mothballs. The Boyd thinks it's too good to go unheard and of course I agree. With no sign of a cinematic release for the actual movie, perhaps putting out the soundtrack will spur things on. By 2001 the writing's on the wall. The wall may have been swept under the carpet, but everybody in the music business knows it's there and they know what's fucking written on it. Artists are getting dropped like hot frogs. Selling rock 'n' roll is like trying to sell a house built from asbestos. It's no use and it will fucking kill you in the end. These days a record can die in the vaults, get everything out there, don't let it rot. With one album release procured thanks to The Boyd's sunny mood, Manager Charlie and I get working on *The Oliver Twist Manifesto.*

'We need one idea. Just one big idea, something to tie in with the release of the record,' ponders DB, lightly tapping his pen on the desk as he thinks. He's thinking of marketing. I'm not.

'Don't worry.' I say. 'I'll come up with something . . .'

*

I write the following in early May 2000. By the end of that month it is published as the cover section of the *Guardian* newspaper's G2 section, with two pages devoted to 'The First National Pop Strike' inside. No editorial, no preceding interview, no context. Just pure manifesto, and one very slow news week.

The First National Pop Strike Manifesto[30]

This manifesto calls upon all pop stars and karaoke singers to down tools and cease to make, distribute, discuss, or perform their 'work'. The term 'pop star' is used here generically to refer to artisans, automata, circus titallantes, pimps, whores, and Illuminati. The idiot savant songwriter must ignore the calling of his muse in the wee small hours. No one is exempt. You, me, and the pop stars are all in this together.

We propose one week of silence from Monday July 2nd 2001, and call for all musicians, all record labels, all live music venues, and all related media to cease activity. During this period there will be no top 40. (Covert listening to already purchased music will be frowned upon but inevitable.) First there was Hear'Say; this is the heresy.

The storming of the Bastille notwithstanding, July is a month not usually associated with insurrectionist activity.

[30] This draft of 'The First National Pop Strike Manifesto' – from the author's archive – may differ from the version that was published in several national newspapers. Also note quaint inclusion of long-forgotten and of-their-time pop acts.

Anti-capitalist riots, Paris '68, and the general strike – all May. Valerie Solanas taking a potshot at the pop art Aunt Sally, Andy Warhol – June. Nevertheless, July will herald the first national Pop Strike. (It is also the month that my new album is released.)

For the purposes of Pop Strike all music is pop music. S Club 7, Schoenberg, Laibach, and Lolly – you are now all equal.

I was recently asked by a London evening paper to pose burning a Steps CD. This is not the point of Pop Strike. A style magazine quoted me as saying Pop Strike is about 'getting rid of all the pop dross'. Getting rid of all the pop dross is not the point of Pop Strike. The new Steps CD is the same as the new Nick Cave CD, is the same as the new Vanessa Mae CD, as the new Starsailor EP, as the second – as yet unrecorded – Moldy Peaches CD. Promotion is relentless. Even my own works of genius such as Baader Meinhof are punted out to restaurants by my own record company. I don't want to listen to Baader Meinhof any more than I want to listen to Judy Garland whilst choking on my sushi.

The more astute or educated reader will by now have noticed that the seeds of the first national Pop Strike can be traced to the art strikes of Gustav Metzger and Stewart Home,[31] *whom I have shamelessly plagiarised here. Metzger*

[31] Stewart Home, artist and writer who sometimes uses long repetitive pornographic sequences for comic conceptual effect and to bolster his word count.

founded auto-destructive art in the late 1950s, whereby buildings, sculptures, and structures would be realised only to be destroyed or to disintegrate. Unsurprisingly, auto-destructive art did not receive much public funding.

In 1977, Metzger called the first international art strike. During a three-year period, artists 'would not produce work, permit work to go on exhibition and would refuse collaboration with any part of the publicity machine of the art world'. Artists being artists, no one came out on strike. The second art strike (1990–93), initiated by the cultural worker Stewart Home, fared better – a handful of artists downed tools. Sadly it failed to bring about the total collapse of the art world. Pop Strike will not fail.

Our aim is to dismantle the apparatus for the music industry, to afford ourselves some peace and quiet, thus enabling us to rethink popular culture. This can only be done in total ascetic silence.

Someone once made the very postmodern claim that 'pop will eat itself'. Well it did, years before Hear'Say. Time to put it out of its misery. One-week trial period. If you miss your fluffy pop bunny you can have it back. Back from the dead. I promised you a miracle; I can deliver.

Alan McGee, Eminem, Badly Drawn Boy, Simon Fuller, Neil Tennant, Cathy Dennis, Geri Halliwell et al – opportunity knocks. I call you all out on a strike action. Cease to be famous. Strike for less pay, socialist musician or scab whore. Join me in silence. This is my altruistic gesture for the world.

All the broadsheets run pieces on the First National Pop Strike, as do the music monthlies. *NME* actually bothers to wheel out a spokesman to announce that it will still be going to press in the first week of July. Good grief.

16

Pop Strike diary

2 July–8 July 2001. A battle to win the hearts and minds of the nation.
Post Everything. Something called 'The Way to Your Love' by Hear'Say. Something called 'Another Chance' by someone called Roger Sanchez, and 'Eternity' – by Black Box Recorder's old label mate Robbie Williams – are all number one singles in the UK charts in July 2001, the month of Pop Strike.

Monday, 2 July. What is supposed to happen: The start of the First National Pop Strike. Remember, no music – of any creed – will be produced, consumed or listened to for seven days. CD pressing plant at Hayes, Middlesex, shuts down. Flying pickets move to smaller independent pressing plants, who are, as ever, slower to grasp the nettle. After initial scab incidents at IPC Tower in South-east London (home to *NME* and various music and pornographic publications), even money-grubbing journos get into line (a few offenders of course). Printing presses grind to a halt. There will be no weekly music press, as sanctioned by the rigid demands of Pop Strike.

What actually happens: Siân and I go down to 'spare' Brighton house (acquired with pop loot from *Facts of Life* success and twin major label record deals). The rules of Pop Strike state clearly that no music is to be consumed or listened to, so in accordance with these rules we do not turn on the radio on the drive down to the seaside. The radio that shouldn't be broadcasting any music anyway. Fucking scabs. On arrival the telephone rings. It's Phill Savidge, my PR – Phill and his business partner John Best pretty much masterminded Britpop, cackling like a pair of demented generals looking down from a hill at the crap carnage below. Phill knows a thing or two about scamming the music industry.

'I've just had the manager of — (useless minnow boy band) on the phone, he's worried that their appearance on *GMTV* is going to be seen as strike breaking.'

'Hahahahaha,' laugh Phill and I in unison.

Tuesday, 3 July. What is supposed to happen: Jarvis Cocker, in full man of the people persona, pickets record shops in Central London before flying up to Sheffield in a Cessna light aircraft, where he will convince simple-minded northern folk to stop shelling out for CDs by launching a pro-nicotine campaign. Our northern brethren, bewitched by a poster of Jarv rakishly puffing on a 555 cig, are easily persuaded to spend the money they would once have frittered on CDs on gaspers instead.

What actually happens: Manager Charlie takes a call from Rough Trade head honcho and well-known left-winger Geoff Travis. Travis will not be supporting Pop Strike as his latest signings, the Strokes, are 'in town'.[32] I put down the phone and watch some tennis on the BBC. This is the safer option as constant ad breaks on ITV/Channel 4 carry the risk of accidental exposure to music. The realisation that it is Wimbledon fortnight on the box is about to hit me hard. I hate tennis. No word from Jarvis.

Wednesday, 4 July. What is supposed to happen: Record sales slump in the north, as a cancerous yellow smog

[32] NOTE TO REVIEWERS. Throughout this chapter I am of course being heavily ironic. I didn't actually expect any pop stars to go on strike, and I didn't expect or even really want the music industry to down tools. In fact I was certain from the off that the First National Pop Strike would fail. The whole thing was just a gag, an exercise in stretching the old imagination: a what if . . . I did, however, observe the strike as an exercise of will power if nothing else. The mentions of Geoff Travis and Jarvis are emphatically not 'scathing attacks' on the individuals concerned. More a gentle poke in the ribs. I certainly would not expect either of them to down tools because I said so; obviously, given Geoff's well-known political leanings, I was asking the impossible of him. That being the point of Pop Strike. In my last book, *Bad Vibes: Britpop and My Part in Its Downfall*, several reviewers noted that I had made a 'scathing' attack on Thom Yorke from Radiohead, by mentioning 'hard rock' and 'fright wigs'. Incorrect, this was not a 'scathing attack'; in 1993, Radiohead were to all intents and purposes leaning towards hard rock, and the singer sported a fright wig. Man, we all sported fright wigs in 1993, I know I did. If any reviewers need help identifying a 'scathing attack' I would point them to the chapter in this book entitled 'Sausage Nuremberg'. Here, even the most short-sighted critic will easily locate a 'scathing attack'.

hangs over Lancashire and Yorkshire; visibility is so poor that flights from Manchester airport are suspended. In the less gullible south, punters are still snaffling what remains in the CD racks. On the plus side, Pop Strike has had some effect on the collective conscience of the nation's hip young things: an official survey reveals that since the beginning of the week no new bands have been formed, and in fact several really big groups are considering calling it a day.

What actually happens: 50,000 terrible new groups have been formed (as they are every other week) and no one is considering packing it in. Flights come and go from Manchester Airport as normal. I sneak out and read a very good review of my album *The Oliver Twist Manifesto* by Paul Morley. Morley gives the record the full five-star treatment; I walk back home and wonder if Paul Morley wakes up screaming at night and if he still really likes Kid Creole and the Coconuts. Realise by looking at a music magazine I have broken the Strike. Go home and watch some more fucking tennis. Man, it's hard trying to avoid all this music. Conclude that Primal Scream are probably not observing Pop Strike.

Thursday, 5 July. What is supposed to happen: The south has finally got the hang of this Pop Strike malarkey. All across the nation cigarette sales go through the roof. Workers at Ford, Dagenham, come out in industrial action in sympathy with the pop stars. Postal workers are also out, but this is unrelated to Pop Strike.

What actually happens: I consider buying a pet, then I think about those posters, 'A dog isn't just for Christmas . . . or Pop Strike.' Obviously I wouldn't be buying a dog anyway. More tennis on the Beeb. Consider travelling to Wimbledon and setting fire to myself on Centre Court. All sports played by men in short trousers are vile. Useless minnow unnamed boy band fulfil their promotional duties on *GMTV*, and there is still no word from Jarvis. Oh, and the bloody post is on strike.

Friday, 6 July. What is supposed to happen: In a televised speech to the nation, the Prime Minister warns striking pop stars that they must return to work by Monday. He makes it clear that if necessary he will call upon the services of the army. The PM neglects to mention postal workers in his tough talk. Civil disorder breaks out in parts of Hertfordshire as striking pop stars engage in violent running battles with non-striking pop stars. Sadly no one is seriously injured.

What actually happens: I take a walk around the shops in Brighton. I wonder if there is in-store music piped into Millets.

Saturday, 7 July. What is supposed to happen: Four striking pop stars are hauled before a hastily convened revolutionary council of war. The pop stars have been accused of covertly trying to blag on to the Strokes' guest list for their show at the Shepherds Bush Empire the following Tuesday. The pop stars are found guilty and will be punished accordingly. This kind of rule break is a serious offence. More worryingly this is a sign that the cracks in Pop Strike are beginning to show. Fucking pop stars, what are they good for?

What actually happens: Yep, as I suspected – there is

piped music in Millets. Good job I don't need a tent. Fucking pop stars, what are they good for?

Sunday, 8 July. What is supposed to happen: Time to take stock. Though it will be years before we can properly assess the significance of this momentous Pop Strike, it is clear that popular culture has had the overhaul it so badly needed. Our minds have been cleansed, for one week we have been on a higher plane, unencumbered by tatty unrequested noise pollution. The machine has been damaged beyond repair, the spanners stick out like honourable apache arrows. The gravy train is fucked, nothing will ever be the same again, bro. As all this has been going on Bill Drummond[33] has been carefully taking notes.

What actually happens: Man, I'm irritable, all this music dodging is fucking hard work. It's more wearing trying to avoid the background hum than it is just surrendering to it. So I've obviously proved something about the power of subliminal auto-suggestion. Still, I've only broken this damned strike a couple of times (accidentally and unavoidably). Stupid. Fucking. Pop. Strike. At least the bloody tennis finishes today. Still no word from Jarvis.

[33] In 2006 Bill Drummond calls for a national no-music day.

17

Under heavy manners at the coalface of light entertainment

August–September 2001. A rotten demo and the unstoppable march to become the nation's new pop idol.
Post Everything. Kylie releases 'Can't Get You Out of My Head', a record that possibly only exists to send ailing music critic Paul Morley irreversibly mental. Hapless Morley will go on to write an entire book about this record. It's a good thing Eno wasn't involved. Pop impresario Jonathan King is convicted on charges of indecent assault – the creator of 'Johnny Reggae' is sentenced to seven years' imprisonment.

Before bringing down the infrastructure of the Western economy with the First National Pop Strike, work, and boy, is it work, has commenced on the third Black Box Recorder album. By the end of the previous year I have squeezed the tube of toothpaste and snatched a decent enough advance out of our label. Even I am surprised; by employing a pincer tactic of obnoxious public 'cunt' calling and steely intransigent psychic warfare, I have coerced Nude label boss, Saul Galpern, into digging deep into those long pockets and pulling out a handsome all-in recording budget and advance of £100,000, almost five times more than the amount we received for *The Facts of Life.* However much we do not spend in the studio, we, the band, get to keep. Saul obviously knows something that we don't. The initial sessions for the album are a drag. Black Box Recorder are no longer definable as a cosy 'art house trio' – we are now redefined as a cosy art house couple and a fucking art house gooseberry. John Moore and I do not really write as a team any more – we just bolt opposing ideas together and cross our fingers. By the time of the group's first recording sessions for the new album, Nixey and Moore are spliced and expecting their first child. On one hand this is a happy time and as JM and SN are my friends I too am happy for them. On the other hand, this is a massive drag. Last time I looked I wasn't in a band with a married couple. Now I'm just a spare prick in a recording studio.

Come September we are preparing for what I hope will be the last BBR recording sessions. I am in the basement of my Camden flat putting the finishing touches to a demo. Some piece of pseudo-sophisticated junk called 'Girl's Guide for the Modern Diva' – it sounds like Ian Hislop has taken an evening class in songwriting, it's woeful stuff for sure. Over the preceding months the album hasn't just moved on a step from *The Facts of Life*, it has jumped off the fucking precipice – we are now struggling to keep a head above water in the rapids of glib, overly arch, and too-knowing-for-its-own-good 'pop'. 'Girl's Guide for the Modern Diva' is a song that seems to exist merely as a lame sort of play on words around 'girl's guide' almost being 'the Girl Guides'. Almost. I try and put to the back of my mind the lacerating fact that Moore and I once exercised our wits by writing 'Child Psychology' and 'The English Motorway System' and get on with the job in hand: recording the dreadful backing vocals to this fluff. I take a deep breath and do my worst – *This is the guide, this is the girl's guide . . . girl's guide for the modern diva, girl's guide for the modern diva, la la la, la la la. . .* I trill pointlessly. After an hour or so of this private humiliation, and having conclusively failed to 'nail' my performance, I decide I need a break. I put on my coat for a wander around the manor on this cold early September afternoon. I speak to Siân on my travel blower as I duck around a more deserted than usual Camden Town. She is a few miles away in Central London, where after being commissioned to write the accompanying book, she is attending and observing auditions for a new TV talent show called *Pop Idol*. As I ring off I catch some excitable conversation from passing foreign exchange students, *Murmur murmur . . . planes . . . New York . . . World Trade Center . . . terrorist attack*. I decide to head home and catch the end of the lunchtime news, but as I walk through the front door thoughts of planes and carnage leave me as I remember the grim incompleted task. The television news can wait. I roll up my sleeves and head straight down to the basement. *This is the guide, this is the girl's guide, girl's guide for the modern diva, girl's guide for the modern diva, la la la, la la la.*

David Boyd – The Boyd – has been a sport, though I wonder if sometimes he teeters on that invisible line between inspiration and haplessness. Perhaps this is just a by-product of being stuck with me, but then he could have got shot many years ago; he has after all been ruthless in the past. There have been plenty who have stood on the trap door at Hut Records to be fed to the crocs, but I'm still here. Maybe The Boyd just enjoys the roller-coaster ride. If that's the case, and if right now he's in the driving seat, then I'm not sure whether we're heading up or down. First, *The Oliver Twist Manifesto* is released and he goes along with my cockeyed Pop Strike idea, then my soundtrack album for *Christie Malry's Own Double-Entry* is finally released; not two months after *The Oliver Twist Manifesto*, not one month after *The Oliver Twist Manifesto*, but two whole weeks after *The Oliver Twist Manifesto*. So let's just tally that up. In July 2001 I have released an album and told people that they must not buy it, I have then released another album two weeks later that is the soundtrack to a film that has not yet been released. David Boyd. A & R genius? A & R lunatic? Both of these albums go on to sell in significantly minuscule amounts.[34]

I've given my all to 'Girl's Guide for the Modern Diva',

[34] In just over a year's time I will be held to account for *The Oliver Twist Manifesto* and the First National Pop Strike by the top brass of Virgin/EMI.

so I conclude that in the worst way possible this demo recording is unimprovable. Just as I am about to abandon ship, the travel blower starts bouncing excitedly on the table. A 'text message' from John Moore. I squint at the tiny fucking screen. 'It must be Gary Numan and Alex James.' OK, it's some sort of ropey flying-based gag. I know the cheery Blur bass player has recently acquired a pilot's licence; on one particularly cheery night out he has even threatened to 'take me up' in his tiny aeroplane. He won't have to worry, I'll never take him up on his kind offer. Then I put Old Moore's text message and the overheard conversation between the exchange students together, and I turn on the television.

My first thought is to phone my wife, who is in Central London. As I dial the number I watch the live news coverage of smoke billowing from the Twin Towers, and listen to the unconfirmed reports of no-fly zones, fighter jet crews being scrambled and the speculation that more planes may be on their way to more targets in other cities. As all this is going on there is another atrocity taking place in London W1: the *Pop Idol* auditions. All morning Siân has sat with a notebook and pen watching auditionee after auditionee warbling their way through the hits of the day. By early afternoon the news from New York has even seeped into this particular ground zero of light entertainment; there is even a rumour amongst some of the more aware pop idolers that planes of death are heading towards London. Of course none of this will interrupt the journey towards stardom. Siân and I finish our phone conversation – she is under heavy manners to go back to work, making notes on more hopeless pop-ees, and catching interviews with the ever-eager hopeless hopefuls. The torrent of light entertainment cannot be stopped. *Apocalypse Now!* may be, er, now! but we still need to find the new pop idol.

18

Our future depends on the future of the man in the gorilla mask

October–November 2001. Not so great apes, The New Avengers, *and life in the last months of Planet Earth.*
Post Everything. Pulp release their final album, We Love Life. *7 October Allied air strikes against Afghanistan. Anthrax attacks across USA. Richard Madeley quite possibly regretting dismantling of 'Millennium cupboard'. George Bush signs executive order allowing military tribunals for foreigners suspected of terrorist acts against the US. Kathleen Soliah, one-time member of Patty Hearst-bothering Symbionese Liberation Army, withdraws her previous guilty plea. Timing is everything. Spice Girls announce an 'indefinite hiatus'. Once again, timing . . .*

In the aftermath to the 11 September attacks people are jumpy, more so than ever before. Low-flying planes making their final descent into Heathrow are viewed with reborn terror eyes by the traffic below on the M4; other forms of attack are imminent: chemical, nerve gas, germ warfare . . . anthrax. October becomes international anthrax month: traces of the stuff – hideously inconvenient white powder – are turning up everywhere, from Delaware to Tinytown. Cocaine consumption hits rock bottom at the Groucho Club and Soho House – no one wants to snort up a nosebag of sheep death. There is just a teensy-weensy bit of hysteria in the air. Then there is the ritualistic rooting out of the new boogie man, Osama someone or other, ah what the fuck, that name will never catch on. A brief moment of levity is achieved when tabloid newspapers learn that this Osama fucker spends most of his time crawling through a network of caves, has a kindly face, and is apparently quite a hit with ladies of a certain age. The levity is followed by war. In Afghanistan. No one has won a war in Afghanistan before, no one will win this war. In fact there are two unwinnable wars going on simultaneously (soon there will be a third), the aforementioned one and a new one: the War on Terror. Now the Britpop Prime Minister and his reluctantly Britpopping War Cabinet can really puff up and show us what they're made of, which is unfortunately exactly what they do. In the months (and years) after the Twin Towers, to see the newly appointed Foreign Secretary, Jack Straw, strutting around thinking he is the Duke of Wellington is the chance to see a man for whom the words *has no self-awareness* were surely invented. You see, this shower aren't fit to be leaders of men, they don't have the necessary militaristic chops. They are university-educated baby boomers, wondering whether that oh so longed for toke on a damp and floppy J will ever jump back to bite them on the long and winding path of ambition. It's a long way from uni, all of this. A long way from Ugly Rumours and bad covers of 'Brown Sugar' ('Gimme Shelter' may have been preferable). Did this Prime Minister really think he was going to have to turn into such a shit-kicker when, in what seems like a lifetime ago, he was taking tea with Alan McGee? Does N. Gallagher still believe himself and aforementioned McGee to be, alongside the gurning, then incoming PM, 'One of the five most important people in the country?' With great power comes responsibility, and on the question of military matters, what exactly is the guy's track record? Christ, this weasel doesn't look like he could take responsibility for a battalion of Action Men. Luckily, he won't have to. In the coming weeks that lead to air strikes against Afghanistan, our man – no, make that *your* man, or *their* man, certainly not *my* man – realises that he won't need to do much shit-kicking. In fact all he will need to do is say yes, and that really suits him; for the one absolute that this PM knows better than anyone else is there is only ever one top dog, and in this case the unassailable top dawg is the President of the United States of America. 'Yes, Mr President.' So once the Britpop PM realises that all he has to do is invoke God and stand tall alongside Mr President, he gets a new look in his eye. It's the same look that Martin McGuinness gets as his brain freezes over in banality whenever the IRA gets a mention. But the IRA have long gone, and this is a very different cell of morons they would have you believe. Terrorists are now everywhere, in the attic, in the cupboards, in the B & B down the road (they would have you believe), and this is nothing like the 'halcyon' days of the 70s and 80s when the Irish dunces held regular bombing campaigns on mainland Britain. Nothing like it. That's what they would have you believe. They walk the walk, this lot, sort of 'Oi, Straw, do I have to tell you again, stop fucking mincing, now drop and give me 50 press-ups', and they give some sort of talk – Islam this, Islam that, cities that we've never heard of before become household names: Islamabad? I should cocoa. So there is all of this, and probably so much more, in the aftermath. But I don't take much notice – not because I am still trying to finish a demo of 'Girl's Guide for the Modern Diva', but because I am happier than I have ever been.

After the Pop Strike, Siân and I spend most of our time in Brighton, where in the town of lazybones we spend our weekdays lolling around on the beach in the September sun. I have become a character in a Ray Davies song – a rich idle rock star, with two houses, a sports car, and no prospects. (I also have a fairly acute case of writer's block.) I figure that the best thing to do is enjoy my aimlessness, enjoy the fulfilment of End Times prophecy. I am in love and love beats everything – even Armageddon – hands down.

Black Box Recorder, meanwhile, are busy – busy putting the finishing touches to our third album. It's not exactly a record that bears any sign of being informed by the onset of Judgement Day, quite the opposite. In the months and years after the World Trade Center attacks, broadsheet newspapers will dribble on in earnest prose (pages damp with clammy sweat wrung out from itchy nervous palms), wondering what the 'artistic response' to 11 September will be: not much, is the answer, a couple of plays and, you'd never guess, an Oliver Stone movie.[35] For all their faults, and they are many, there is a perfectly good reason why artists are artists and critics are critics: artists don't always take the bait. Critics do. With. Out. Fail – and without exception. It's still a jaw dropper. BBR hand in our work to the record company and sit and wait. Actually, we're pretty pleased with ourselves.

Not without reason. The album, eventually to be titled *Passionoia*, is pretty good. OK, 'pretty good' sounds like faint praise, but, on completion, if the ten tracks are not exactly watertight as a complete statement, then they do work a lot better together than on their own, with at least two killer songs amongst their number: 'British Racing Green', mainly written by John, and slightly taking the piss out of my newfound sports car ownership, and 'The New Diana', mainly written by me, and which for some reason was a struggle to get past 'The Other Two'. The rest of the album exists in its own world of turbo-ironic supercharged 'pop'. Electronic chimes crackle and a toy beat box purchased from Argos emits tiny-horse drums and silly cuddly toy squeaks as Sarah Nixey slays the populace like Purdey from *The New Avengers*. Even the loathed (by me at least) 'Girl's Guide . . .' sounds feasible in this context. Hell, if the New Avengers had made a record then that record would be *Passionoia*. The label like the album as well, and think it an ideal follow-up

[35]And *Heathen*? Bowie's last decent album (albeit with relentlessly stupid bass sound).

to *The Facts of Life*. In strange days such as these, pop music is often given to the escapist knee-jerk reflex, and by the end of 2001 the flow is towards the ultra-ironic: electro-clash, apparently a nanosecond genre that refers to bands who, shall we say, have a strong Giorgio Moroder element to their music. Fischerspooner, a New York duo, are the perhaps unwilling pioneers of this nebulous movement.[36] The poor sods have been signed for an amount somewhere between 46 pence and 72 gazillion bucks, depending on who you speak to, and one of them dresses up as an ape (this is a good thing). According to those who know about such things (this is nobody), the 'Spooner are going to do the business like no one has ever done the business before. I have a strong feeling of déjà vu. Anyway, this is all supposed to be good news for Black Box Recorder, because according to our record label we fit right in with this new 'scene'. It is great at the age of 34 to be told that you are at the cutting edge of something that you've previously not heard of, especially when you have a strong instinct that this particular something might be about as cutting edge as a pair of child-friendly scissors, and is as secure in its place in the pop firmament as the string on a birthday balloon on a windy day in the light clasp of a toddler's fingers. With all this in mind it is decided that the new BBR album should come

[36] Whenever it is announced that there is a new musical movement/trend/scene you can bet your mother's liver that the 'perpetrators' of said movement/trend/scene consider themselves far removed from that particular albatross which is gleefully being attached to their not so broad shoulders.

out as soon as possible in the New Year. *Why not*, I think to myself, *go with it? You feared the worst for this album and now you are quite fond of it, perhaps it is entirely appropriate that the future of this record rests in the luckless hands (paws) of two men dressed as apes*. We are living in strange times indeed.

Then comes November. The planes over the M4 seem to get lower, the drivers of the cars below seem more nervous, and the fog of war gets denser. The world's first light entertainment PM is now coming across as a weird Kim Jong-Il/ Lionel Blair hybrid who seems to think he has a direct line to King Arthur; unfortunately we all know who he has a direct line to. And despite all the posturing, and give or take a few of the old guard of MPs who are currently being kept very busy in their constituencies, there is not a single member of this bloody Cabinet who can do a convincing line in macho. Throughout this dreadful and interesting time of human misery/history, we three Black Box Recorders are sitting pretty, three dysfunctional shamen of irony perched on a magic carpet. We are pleased (enough) with our work, and when Nude Records pays us the remainder of the advance, we are once again affluent. Siân and I whizz up and down the motorway in our fabulous sports car between our two pop star homes in London and Brighton. These are the days of expensive clothes, champagne, and parties – this must be what it felt like being Bryan Ferry in 1973. Except this is better – this is like being Bryan Ferry (in 1973) and the world is about to end. Hahaha. This really is the best of times and the worst of times . . . it's *Vile Bodies*, it's *Goodbye to Berlin* . . . and it lasts for about a couple of weeks, then the magic carpet is pulled from beneath our irrelevant little tootsies.

Mid-November 2001. I am lording it up on a Thursday lunchtime in our Brighton swank-pad. I have just booked in for afternoon tea at the Grand Hotel. Within seconds of me replacing the receiver the phone rings again. This is highly unusual, no one rings this number, it's kind of off limits.

'Have I got news for you,' says Manager Charlie. This is a coded phrase: he uses it when there is no good news. Whenever 'Have I got news for you' issues forth from the other end of the ear trumpet it means, 'We do not need to exchange pleasantries, they will only lead us off on a conversational tangent. There is bad shit on the horizon and now is the time to address it.'

'What's going on?' I ask, with all the enthusiasm of a man who knows he is about to have his day/week/month/year ruined.

'It's your record label.'

'Which one?' I say, savouring my retort perhaps a little too much.

'Nude,' says Manager Charlie. 'They've run into problems.' I make a mental note to cancel afternoon tea at the Grand. I can see we are rapidly heading towards a day-ruined situation, but I still have hope. Sorry, did I just say 'hope'? Pity the poor naïve fool. We have been here before: it is not untypical for Nude or any record label to run into 'problems' – most record labels are not just on first-name terms with chaos, they are in a torrid threesome with incompetence and stupidity. Only 18 months ago, just as 'The Facts of Life' single was about to be released, Nude promptly lost its own deal with parent company Sony. For a few awkward days it looked as if our one-hit wonder was never going to be.

'It's a bit different from the last time this happened,' continues Manager Charlie, in a disconcerting manner, having followed my train of thought via telepathy. 'Nude Records are in administration.'

Yep, we have hurtled through the 'day ruined' situation, not even stopping to wave hello to 'week ruined', landing bang on starters orders for 'month ruined'.

'You better explain it all to me,' I sigh wearily to Manager Charlie.

'You better sit down,' he says.

'Year ruined' situation. It transpires that Nude Records owes a lot of money to a lot of people. The people it owes money to are called creditors. One of its creditors is the Inland Revenue. If there is one body that you don't want to get into debt with it is the Inland Revenue. Actually you can't get into debt with the Inland Revenue. If you do you will be shut down. It is time for Nude Records to stop trading. The company will go into administration, and all the company's assets will be in the hands of the receivers. Nude's assets are everything it owns. The assets will be sold off to pay the creditors what they are owed. That is the theory at least. At first, it looks like the worst thing that could happen to BBR is that we will not be paid the remainder of our advance and we will be free to seek out a new record label to release our album. Scant knowledge. In fact our album will become part of the holding company's assets: we will have to wait for all the legal loose ends to be tied up before these assets – which would include previously released albums on the label like *The Facts of Life*, office furniture, promotional items, the master tapes for our new album, *Passionoia*, and Saul's dog Marnie[37] – can be put up for auction. There is a further complication to all this: because of a clause in our record contract, whoever ends up buying Nude's assets will not be allowed to release our album (a) without our consent, and (b) without paying us the outstanding advance. The most likely outcome will be that whoever ends up with Nude Records' old tat is unlikely to want to deal with BBR's contractual stipulations. In short, Black Box Recorder are not legally allowed to sign a new record deal. We can seek out interested parties but we are not allowed to enter into a contract with any new business suitors until all the asset-stripping has been done. When not a soul alive – our lawyer, the administrators, the administrator's lawyers – will even hazard a guess as to how long this process could take, you know that you and the devil are in some deep shit together. I'm not entirely confident that electro-clash and the men from New York dressed as apes will still be going strong by the time our 'new' album comes out, but against this tangle of red tape, legalese, and foreboding administration addresses of units in industrial estates in Brentwood, I'm not sure even *The New Avengers* would have stood much chance.

[37] I am joking of course.

19

We are Tuesday, or, Have I got news for you (Slight return)

Late November 2001. One last blag under the noses of a coup d'état.

Post Everything. Taliban prisoner John Walker Lindh is found to be an American citizen. Deaths include Ken Kesey and George Harrison. First series of Pop Idol *begins. Gareth Gates and Will Young will get to duke it out on the final. Damn straight.*

'Have I got news for you,' sing-songs Manager Charlie wearily down the phone approximately two weeks after the last time he uttered the dread phrase.

'What's happened?' I ask, although I'd rather not know the answer.

'David Boyd has just called, he doesn't think he's going to be allowed to put out any more of your records.'

'That sounds rather like I'm being dropped.'

'I'm not sure. It's not good though, let me come over and tell you what I know, then we'll go over to Hut, David wants to see us in his office.'

Indeed, this is not good. Just one month ago, Manager Charlie and I had one of our 'good' meetings with The Boyd. Under discussion was a new film soundtrack for an independent French film. DB was all up about the soundtrack and full of encouragement, promising to help out with recording budgets (the musical score to an independent film is often lowest on the list of financial considerations to a film production company, so the actual recording budget can sometimes be minuscule). Since that happy meeting, the French film has fallen through, Black Box Recorder's new album is being held for ransom at the receivers, and now the rumblings emanating from Dave Boyd's cave are pitch-black.

Well, there are worse things than losing record deals, I just wasn't planning on losing both record deals in the same week. But I know a secret: I may be sailing fucking close to the wind, but I am not about to get dropped. Because today is Tuesday – no one in the world ever got dropped on Tuesday. If you are unlucky (or lucky) enough to get dropped, you will be summoned on a Friday. Here's the drill for Friday droppage: record label calls up manager on Friday lunchtime for nice friendly meeting. Manager thinks he's been invited in for smashing end of week drug and debauchery session. Come end of play manager leaves record company HQ undrugged and label-less. The only thing he has got for his trouble is his tail between his legs, and a shitload of Bob Bad News to relate to his young idiot charges (the group). Grim tidings will be strategically withheld from young idiot charges until Friday evening, when of course it will be too late to march into the record company offices shouting the odds. Young idiot charges will vow to take their revenge on Monday. This will never happen as by Monday the group (the idiot charges) will have split up. The record company will have signed and bought instruments for a brand spanking new bunch of young idiot charges (fresh group) out of the money they would have spent on the dropped idiot charges, and by teatime the whole thing will be forgotten. Leaving us at Tuesday, the day when all the lovely happy meetings take place. I know this, even if Manager Charlie does not. We are safe, we are Tuesday.

Two hours later. My confidence concerning the rule of Tuesday is a little wobbly. Manager Charlie and I sit in the large reception of Virgin/EMI HQ, Kensal House. I have sat here a hundred times before, sometimes anticipating bad news, other times safe in the knowledge that the meeting is going to be a gas. But now the psychic atmosphere in the building is different. In late 2001 the war on terror may be rumbling along apace, but inside this building an ancient conflict is being resumed: the war against the old enemy – the French. And we don't stand a fucking chance. The French have taken over, that is, a French company has taken over Virgin/EMI – and there's a massacre going on. The music industry is terminally ill, CD sales are down, and there's a file-sharing epidemic on the internet that just cannot be cured. The French solution to all this is to kick the shit out of the old place: bands are being dropped like oily eggs, people are losing their jobs, and the building reeks of distrust, fear, and ultimately defeat. The general feeling is that if you are in some way connected with this building, right here, right now in November 2001, then come New Year all ties will be severed. I lean back on the leather reception chair and feel a knife making an enquiry of my lung. I lean forward again quick smart. I've gauged the fucked atmosphere and I'm not so sure the rule of Tuesday still counts.

The Boyd beckons us in. He's friendly enough but I can see the tension in his eyes. The first thing to report is that the Hut office has shrunk, and the whole operation has also moved down a few floors. When I signed to this label back in 1992, it was on the top floor, up in the attic – just two rooms with a low ceiling. A funny little enterprise sneaking through Pussy Galore and Royal Trux records right under the uninterested beak of EMI. By 1997 Dave Boyd had made the label a success and the Hut office sprawled, moving down a few floors occupying the middle of the building. Now, just a few years later, with the arrival of the bloodthirsty French, the Hut operation perches precariously on the first floor. Next stop is out the fucking front door, people.

Fucking Tuesday. We sit around, and David and I talk about the old days, doing our old-campaigner act. The Boyd is righteously angry – the writing's not so much on the wall any more as in every fucking top brass fucking memo. This French shake-up is a crock of merde. I'm not angry, I just feel a little misty-eyed. I'll miss all this – the sparring, the winging it – and I feel genuinely upset for Boyd, who is in all probability going to have the label he lived and breathed shut down. The bigger acts on Hut – Placebo, Ashcroft et al – will be subsumed by EMI, whilst the acts that sell fuck all – me – will be told to fuck off – as will the man who took care of the whole operation. David Boyd. *Merci bien.*

'There's nowhere left to hide,' says David, '. . . for both of us.'

'I know,' I say, 'don't worry about it.' Fucking Tuesday.

DB continues to murmur away sadly in his soft spoken Northern Irish brogue. I'm not really listening, I'm just taking in the situation, then something catches my eye screwed up in the wastepaper bin, a memo that I can't entirely make out and has my name on it.

'. . . But I've got one idea,' says The Boyd looking up conspiratorially and immediately buying my attention back.

'What if you were to do an acoustic album – re-record the old songs – I'm sure I could sneak it through as "back catalogue",' continues David. It's an unbelievable masterstroke. A get-out-of-jail card from the bottom of the back.

'What if I re-record the songs with an orchestra, like those "classic rock" albums they used to advertise on TV,' I add, for luck, thinking on my feet.

'Fuck it, let's give it a go,' says Boyd, plotting. 'I'll put in a budget of 70k, use what you have to record with, and keep any money left over.' It's war. Boyd's war against the French and the company who are about to sell him down the river. None of us say it out loud – on this Tuesday of long knives walls have ears, and we need to move stealthily. We all get up and shake hands, and nod silently. One last blag, fellas. One last great big blag. On my way out I manage to make out the screwed-up memo in the bin. Seven words:

Re Luke Haines – contract to be terminated.

David Boyd, true ally, is having none of it. No seven-word cop-out for him. If I/we have to go let's go with a fucking bang. We cannot possibly win the war, but we can win this battle.

We have the wind in our sails, Manager Charlie and I, as we hurtle down the staircase towards the exit of Kensal House, picking up speed as we get nearer the front door. We came here hoping only for a reprieve of execution. Instead we leave the building 70 grand better off. This is daylight robbery, and we don't stop to talk until we get clear of fucking Virgin Records, some 500 yards up the Harrow Road. Even then we are too breathless with excitement to really speak. But, of course, it's not about the money. It's about David Boyd and me sticking it to the cunts. It's about us showing the top brass, whoever they were and whoever they are, that they will never be able to totally outsmart us. We will always come back at them with something. Remember, when so-called Britpop was making news headlines, we, David Boyd and I, were putting out an album called *Baader Meinhof*. On this very label. We do what we want to, and we do not go quietly. We are Tuesday.

20

The Dave heads

February–June 2002. Recording one final album for Hut after curfew. Tom Verlaine tells a joke. Punk rules and Post Everything non-rules, and being snubbed by a moron.
Post Everything. Robert Mugabe wins Zimbabwe election on 4 March. Dudley Moore dies. The Osbournes *debuts on MTV. Oh Ozzy, what have you done? The Streets release* Original Pirate Material, *and in May Liberty X, winners of TV show* Pop Stars – The Rivals, *release their debut album*, Thinking It Over.

I'd seen Bowie once before – at the Milton Keynes Bowl in the early 80s, on the *Serious Moonlight* tour. Man, it was an atrocity. Pounding slabs of horrible funkoid/jazz/rock cut 'n' shut wafting through the grey early-evening new-town air, as sad, loyal Dave heads wondered if life could possibly get any worse. They'd all tried to like the *Let's Dance* album, but now, seated on man-made grassy mounds, nursing their flimsy plastic pints of lager, the truth was impossible to ignore, as 'Modern Love' entered its tenth minute and 75 miles away the bandana-headed tiny figure of either Earl Slick or Carlos Alomar phoned in the umpteenth FX poodle rock guitar solo. There was no longer any doubt. It was easy to disseminate the duality of fact: *Let's Dance* was of course a floor-filling production tour de force, and a rapid-fire cash machine of an album. It was also a pile of shit. Of course, this was the 80s, and for Dave fans life would get much worse. There would be the 90s. Oh yes, the 90s. But right now, in June 2002, we are over the worst. It's Bowie's Meltdown festival at the South Bank, that strange fake event where an artist pretends to 'curate' a series of concerts. So, on this occasion, the organisers of Meltdown are pretending that Bowie has invited me to play. Of course, what this amounts to is really me making up the numbers by supporting the reheated Television, but what the hell, it's Bowie, I'll play along. Yep, Bowie has invited me to play at Meltdown, he phoned me on a Friday night – I thought it was a friend playing a trick on me (y'know, anyone can do a half-decent Bowie impersonation). I told him that I loved all his 70s albums (even *Pinups*, *David Live*, and *Stage*), but I had to go against popular opinion so I told him that *Scary Monsters* was a sack of cack. David laughed at my impudence but said that on the whole he agreed. Before he rang off he emotionally told me how much my work meant to him.

'See you at sound check, big guy,' I said as I put the phone down, David Bowie's high praise still ringing in my ear.

*

Tom Verlaine, 'Blitzkrieg maverick lead guitarist of seminal symbolist New York City art rockers'[38] and one time most intense man in rock, pokes his head around my dressing room door and points directly at me. The hand is instantly recognisable, from the canals of protruding veins that leapt out of the sleeve of *Marquee Moon*. These are the hands after all that led Julian Cope to invite the one time Tom Miller to produce him. Cope had concluded that anyone with veins like that must be, well, *intense*.

'Two words,' says Tom Verlaine owlishly over his glasses, letting the door hold his still gangly frame, not entering the room.

'Huh?' I manage.

'Bowie song. Two words?' booms the singer from Television, intensely.

'Rebel Rebel,' I shoot back. With that Tom Verlaine is off, for a less than perfunctory run-through of *Marquee Moon*. My own Meltdown performance is OK, the real

[38] My own words to describe Verlaine and Television, as used in my first book, *Bad Vibes: Britpop and My Part in Its Downfall*. Of course, in the 1990s/2000s the reformed Television and their ilk (I'm talking about you Iggy, Devoto, Dolls, P.Orridge et al) have lost all dignity and more importantly they have pissed their own considerable mythology up against the wall. For my mob – moulded in the precious and notoriously picky mid-80s independent scene – *Marquee Moon* was sacrosanct, and its follow-up, *Adventure*, nothing less than a noble failure. These records did not deserve a half-cocked third album years later, as a kind of afterthought to a bunch of ailing solo 'careers' and the depressingly inevitable live outings for the debased necrophiled corpse. Uh uh, no way.

highpoint being when the 'Death of Sarah Lucas' attracts a few heckles. I'd thrown it into the set as a kind of low-grade homage to Bowie's own 'Andy Warhol', but I'd forgotten that Dave was a fully paid-up champion of the Brit Art crowd. Man, the glory years were a long time ago, and that is what it is all about. In the spirit of all things South Bank-ish and twenty-first century the main reason for being involved in this Bowie Meltdown is that three days after my own insignificant performance I get the chance to watch Big Dave perform *Low* in its entirety. That's *Low.* Of course, the guitarist will probably have the wrong guitar sound, and there'll be slap bass, and the Mary Hopkin vocals on 'Sound and Vision' will be performed by some vocal gymnast session singer, and he's also going to be performing all of the new album too, and there's loads of keyboards on *Low*, and he definitely won't be using all the rickety original synths, so he's going to have to use horrible modern keyboards, so it will most likely have the wrong keyboard sound, and God forbid if he wears anything like that Union Jack frockcoat which he wore on the cover of some grim album a few years ago. So there are many reasons why this may suck on dead dogs' dicks. But it is *Low*, and that may be enough to get the Dave heads – of which I most certainly am one – through.

The early months of 2002 are schizophrenic. The grand caper with Hut Records – the more I think about it the more improbable it seems – takes months to sanction. I start to wonder whether the meeting where Dave Boyd, Manager Charlie, and I planned a coup d'état against the bastard French actually happened, could it be something that I dreamt up? Perhaps I have actually been dropped and I'm just in a state of denial. In the weeks after the meeting, as strange 2001 withers away, the phone line between The Boyd and Manager Charlie remains silent. I busy myself doing some film soundtrack work, hoping that DB will break cover. Nothing. With Black Box Recorder's album still in legal purgatory and no word from our man behind enemy lines, the future looks barren. Then finally, on the worst day of fucking February, Manager Charlie gets the call from The Boyd.

He's fucking done it. That Irish mutherfucka has actually gone and done it, we've relieved the fucked Virgin/EMI of £75,000. We almost get rumbled at the final hurdle, when a French executive takes DB aside and asks exactly why the company are about to shell out £75,000 on an artist whose contract has been terminated; the bizarre 'back catalogue' clause is invoked by Le Boyd and the French executive is sniffily satisfied. The budget is green-lighted. With some haste I make arrangements to hire string players, woodwinds, and brass. Even if I can't quite stretch to a full orchestra, it's still got to be epic. Studio time must be booked quickly – this is all a gamble; at any time the French could realise that they've been had. Get the money in the bank, get the record done quickly, pay everyone quickly, keep your mouth fucking shut.

The album I am about to record feels like it was conceived in the illicit Post Everything hinterland, so the script is amorphous, and Post Everything you can do what you like, there are – as was always meant to be the way – no rules.

The most adhered-to rock rulebook was written just after that great leap of the imagination – punk – had crossed into the mainstream. By the time tricky Dicky Branson released the Sex Pistols album in late '77, the tablets had been handed down from the mountain, and the Ten Commandments were observed and obeyed by all.

1 No flares.
2 No long hair.
3 No songs over three minutes.
4 If you are 20 you're too old.
5 Nihilism rules – remember Malcolm McLaren's odious 'She's dead – I'm yours' Sid Vicious T-shirt after the death of Nancy Spungen.
6 Stupidity rules – the Clash.
7 Everything is fast – remember, detail will betray you.
8 Everything is bad – the worse you are, the nearer you are to achieving your aim: misery and death.
9 You are living in year zero – everything that came before is boring or, at best, to be mistrusted, but crucially everything that isn't 'punk' is that most hated of all things: hippy.
10 There are no rules.

Punk became a major drag, and its commandments were rigidly maintained into the 80s. The tablets were eventually smashed into shards at the end of that decade by irony. But irony, just like the punk rules, was another dead weight. But punk didn't start out to be a rigid albatross, no, sir, witness the wild leaps of imagination of Subway Sect, with their skeletal noise and lyrics cut up from 'essays'. The Sect sounded like a rusty galleon being hurled around in a hurricane. Post punk before anyone had even worked out what punk was 'supposed to be'. *We oppose all rock and roll.* Damn straight. And then there was the Bromley Contingent, and Sid's first group with future Slit Viv Albertine, The Flowers of Romance, and of course the Pistols' early noise/scream blood curdler, 'Flowers', but Johnny never made much of a secret of the fact that he was really a teenage head who dug Hawkwind, Peter Hammill, and Beefheart. Jeez, even the Damned knew there were no rules until Brian James wanted out. Then there was the Clash.[39]

[39] After Joe Strummer's sad death in 2002, and his inevitable canonisation culminating in Julien Temple's film, *Joe Strummer: The Future Is Unwritten*, which seemed to set out to portray its subject as a kind of Lennon-ised, Marley-fied Joe Public, but ended up making him look more like Joe Stalin, it has been hard (for me at least) to retain much fondness for the Clash. In 1980, I was a 13-year-old Clash fan – punk took a long time to hit some of the UK's less metropolitan cities, in my case Portsmouth. Bored by the major drag that was *London Calling* – even my early teenage ears had sussed that the guitars were way too low in the mix, and why was Paul Simonon singing like a lobotomised Sting on the truly idiotic 'Guns of Brixton?' – precocious teeny me knew that the Clash's money shot was always going to be *Give 'Em Enough Rope*, the derided second album. Thirty years later and the damned record is still seen as the jackknifed truck of the Clash's career. And I'm still right. Sure, 'Janie Jones' is a great opener to that debut album, but can anybody now listen to all that no-shit-Sherlock crock about

March 2002. Express work begins on the album that will become *Das Capital*, making full use of the Post Everything maxim: that we are beyond rules. The sessions that stretch out for a period of about three weeks are carried out in an atmosphere of anticipation and tension; at any time I suspect that the French may send an agent to close us down. The album will of course become a meta 'greatest hits' collection, but there are no greatest hits, there won't even be any original recordings of the old songs, everything will be bathed in sheer opulence (or with as much of an orchestra as I can afford). If I want to spray-gun an inferior version of 'Lenny Valentino' with a Moroccan-style string arrangement then I goddamn will. I conclude that at the present rate of 'legendary' groups reforming – quicker than you can

---

fat politicians, being bored, and getting 'nicked for fighting in the road'? Perhaps most revealing was the cover of 'Police and Thieves'; after hearing Junior Murvin's original could the Clash's lead-booted version be described as anything other than musical bricklaying? *London Calling* is still the dog's dinner it always was; more musical sink installation ('Clampdown') misrepresented as a homage to Americana, though *Sandanista* does actually walk it and talk it (despite the usual ridiculous Clash paranoia about being 'called up' by the armed forces). But . . . *Rope*, with Blue Oyster Cult production and Mick Jones's cluster bombing of every track with fabulous Mott-isms, is the closest the Clash ever got to taking the mantle of 'the greatest rock 'n' roll band in ver world', and the closest they got to being the greatest rock 'n' roll gang that they so wanted to be. That their adoring horde of weeping old men choose to ignore all this, in favour of the received wisdom of *London Calling*, is the crying shame of the matter.

say 'pension plan' – then in these less than aesthetically stringent times, I can do no wrong. Even though I am supposed to be re-recording my old songs I have a few new ones that I decide to record as well: 'Satan Wants Me'[40] is a mini-history of the occult, Dennis Wheatley rides out with Scott Walker's version of Brel's 'Jackie'. But best of all is 'The Mitford Sisters', a song that almost collapses under the weight of its epic ambitions: a triptych, no less, that attempts to simultaneously imagine Britain in 1942 under Nazi occupation, a horny fighter pilot ditching his stricken plane, and the lives of Britain's foremost upper-class, romantic, fascism-dabbling dynasty, the Mitford sisters. As I figure that I may not be making any more records for a while I may as well throw everything I've got at 'The Mitford Sisters'. See, no rules. By the end of March the album is completed. I will have to wait for over a year to see if it is actually released.

There was no need to worry, Bowie's rendition of *Low* turns out to be note-perfect – in a good way. The guitar sound isn't as heinous as it could have been, the session singers are on a tight leash, and most importantly there is no sign of the frockcoat atrocity. For some of us, there is an 'intermission', before Bowie takes a run at the dreaded new

[40] Originally written and recorded to be part of the soundtrack to a screen adaptation of the Robert Irwin novel of the same name. The film never got made. The soundtrack album was to be called *Satan Wants Me – Symphony for the Devil*. Shame.

album. For others, like myself, this is the end of the show. *Low* was good, and has done a lot of work in soothing the terrible memories of Milton Keynes Bowl 1983. As I make for the bar I am grabbed by The Drummer Out Of Supergrass. I never minded this lot: the Auteurs supported them in the very early 90s when they were still toddlers and called themselves the Jennifers. The drummer was about three years old and he could still play like Keith Moon on a sugar high.

'Do you wanna meet Bono?' asks The Drummer Out Of Supergrass. Before I can respond with 'No, not really', The Drummer has 'had a word' with a security type and darted off into a cordoned-off area. I presume that I have seen the last of him and my introduction to a man that all sentient beings could surely only ever think of as a nincompoop has been happily derailed. I am wrong. Out of the mists of the VIP area returns The Drummer Out Of Supergrass. He has been successful in his quest, and walking behind him is the tiny, yet oddly puffed-up figure of the extremely silly lead singer out of U2. These situations never play out well. The social balance is cock-eyed from the off. The singer out of U2 will have been told I have requested some kind of audience with him, that I am in some way familiar with his work, and worse still hold him in some regard. Of course, I know next to nothing about this minuscule fucker, I shudder at the memory of some steaming pile of dreck about 'New Year's Day', and that's about it. Showbiz and rock 'n' roll, as any fool knows, are a conspiracy of smoke and mirrors, and the singer out of U2's sleight of hand is to cover his messianic shaman figure in the shroud of the great everyman made good. Fuck that, buster. The singer out of U2's house of cards is held up by one unutterably stupid assertion: that we live in a world without nuance.

'Two words – singer out of U2', as Tom Verlaine might have said. I can only conclude that the two most appropriate words are 'Massive twat.'

Did I mention that these situations never play out well? Somehow, I have been joined by six more people, and we have inadvertently and unconsciously organised ourselves into a kind of reception committee for the singer out of U2. This is not a good place to be. Bono, with The Drummer Out Of Supergrass at his side, works his way down the greeting party, shaking hands and asking questions as if he's fucking royalty. Then he gets to me. I don't offer my hand in earnest but I will do if necessary. I am not without manners, but there is no need. The singer peers at me through his idiot shades, snorts a little, and moves down the line, totally ignoring me. Perhaps he's a mind reader. The Drummer Out Of Supergrass looks embarrassed for me, but there is no need: there is no better feeling in life than being snubbed by a moron.

'Do you wanna meet Bowie?' offers The Drummer Out Of Supergrass.

I only give it a moment's thought.

'No, thanks,' I say.

21

The man from *Rising Damp*

July 2002. Black Box Recorder get their album back, but a 70s sitcom stalwart is not impressed.
Post Everything. Backstreet Boys have had enough and Alan Lomax, folklorist and ethnomusicologist, dies. The two events are unrelated.

The man from *Rising Damp* – the one who had to go along with all that business about being the son of an African prince – looks at me in abject horror. I imagine it must take a fair bit to faze 'Philip', what with Miss Jones's rampant ardour and all those parts he must have been offered as a black comic actor in the unenlightened world of British sitcom in the 1970s. Right now, those days pale into insignificance. The man out of *Rising Damp*, as he stands before me on the pavement, is very angry, actually he is disgusted, and I am as pissed as a cunt.

The *Das Capital* album is in the can, and the master tapes (DATs) sit on a shelf in the ever-diminishing environs of what will soon cease to be Hut Records. The sessions went well and nearly all the songs that have been re-recorded are better than the originals (though I know I'll have a hard job convincing 'the kids' about that one). David Boyd likes this album a lot and hints strongly that he wishes I had taken this path – sonically at least – rather than the *Oliver Twist Manifesto* path, a few years ago. Ah well, Dave, I'm an artist not a career as you well know. I can scam and I can connive (all artists are at the very least borderline criminals), let's just thank the Lord that we have pulled off this caper and be thankful I cannot plan to save my life or yours. This year, 2002, is looking like it is going to be the first year since the Auteurs' debut album, *New Wave*, in '92, that I have not had a full-length album released. I decide that I should compensate by reminding people just what those nitwits in the music press were saying about me, ooh, ten years ago. So I decide that I will title the album that will eventually be released in a little over a year's time *Das Capital – The Songwriting Genius of Luke Haines and the Auteurs*. To celebrate this marvellous accolade that I have bestowed upon myself, I repair to the pub.

You can't beat afternoons in the pub: a couple of pain-killers, a sturdy breakfast, then in the boozer by half eleven, play your hand right and you'll be tucked up safe in bed and sound asleep before the springs hit the floor at 7.30 in the evening. We have followed the drill scrupulously, John

Moore and I, as the glasses pile up on this summer afternoon in our favourite daytime souse-house, the Spread Eagle in Camden Town. We are no longer singing the 'our album's down at the receivers blues', a song we've been singing since last fucking November. At times the song has felt like it may never cease, until finally, in July 2002, the interminable blues workout has at last played itself out. Independent record company One Little Indian has been patiently waiting in the wings for Black Box Recorder's legal woes to come to an end, and we have now put pen to paper with the label, who will release our third album, *Passionoia*, at the beginning of next year. John Moore and I celebrate our release from purgatory in the only sensible way we know – by getting as drunk as we can.

'I've already cleaned these windows once today,' says the ever tolerant landlady of the Spread Eagle pub only half seriously. She's a game old bird and J. Moore doesn't put up much resistance as she gently but firmly moves him away from the window that he has been licking with his tongue. We kid ourselves that the landlady finds our awful drunkenness endearing, but grown men slobbering over windows, I ask you. John Moore is not to be fazed, however, he's found a new way to pass the time, in the twilight of our drunkenness – it involves banging on the window and gesturing to people out on the street that he would like them to come into the pub and fight him. For about five minutes this seems like the best game in the world, until an arrow slit of clarity flits across my blitzed brain, and I realise that asking strangers to fight you on the streets of

Camden Town ain't really that clever. It's been a good day but it's time for me to go home.

Most of the hot dog I have just bought from the street vendor is down the front of my suit; ketchup covers my face like the blood from a mouthful of busted teeth. My wife, who has been called to rescue me from the pub, holds me up. On the pavement in front of me is 'Philip' from *Rising Damp*. One of the things I like about living in Central London is that you run a good chance of being observed by 'famous' people doing things that are bad. This is a far better way of spending your time than trying to spot the successful and well-known: let 'em come to you – and then fuck up in their face. This is precisely what I am doing to 'Philip'. I am fucking up in his face. Radioactive yellow mustard drips from my fingers, and a flaccid frankfurter dislodges itself from its soggy mummy dog bun, falling on the dog-shit Camden Town pavement. 'Philip', who has just had the misfortune to stray into my zig-zagging path, dramatically and slowly looks me up and down, a total, yet awful stranger to him. I raise my hand and point at the actor, but words do not make themselves available to me. I am too drunk to stand and too drunk to talk. 'Philip' wrinkles his nose in disgust, like he's looking at a racist comedy script. The man is truly appalled. He lets out a long derisive snort and barrels past me. There are a lot of drunks in Camden Town, but today I may be one of the worst. I wonder what John is up to as my wife helps me 'walk' the short distance home. Black Box Recorder's album is out of the legal wilderness and I have been royally put down by the phoney African prince of 70s sitcom.[41] I feel strangely good. I go to bed and pass out. Not necessarily in that order.

[41] It is not until the 1980 big-screen spin-off of *Rising Damp* that 'Philip' reveals he is really from Croydon, not Africa.

22

Fucked. Irredeemably

October–November 2002. Christie Malry *gets out of jail. The all-important seating plans of awards ceremonies, and Black Box Recorder choose a single.*
Post Everything. United Nations unanimously approve UN Security Council resolution forcing Saddam Hussein to 'disarm or face serious consequences'. Death of Myra Hindley on 15 November.

Armed with the knowledge that the machinations of the music business are entirely predictable, whilst choosing to entirely ignore this accumulated wisdom, Manager Charlie, myself and The Moore/Nixey hydra are having a 'meeting' with our new record label, One Little Indian. The meeting is ostensibly to plan a strategy for the release of the straight-outta-debtors'-jail Black Box Recorder album *Passionoia*. The worrying part of all this is that I am 'on' my tenth album and the 'strategy' is always the same: choose a single, play a gig, release the album, do some more gigs. Unfortunately, after a year or so out of commission, the not-so-new album, *Passionoia,* sounds peculiarly dated, with its beeps and frightening electronica.

'The kind of group we're really looking to champion would be a kind of hybrid of the New York Dolls and the MC5,'[42] says the dozy *NME* writer in the early autumn of 2002. Good grief. Whilst ignoring the fundamental untruth in this statement – that the *NME* will 'champion' what they

[42] Let's focus on the latter band and kick this faux svengali, king-making statement to death with a bit of Post Everything enlightenment: the MC5 were formed in Lincoln Park, Michigan, in the mid-60s, starting out, as so many US garage bands did, in thrall to the British beat invasion of the Who and The Kinks. They did not deliberately, as bozo from the *NME* seems to think, set out to become the Proto-Hard-Rock-Righteous-Free-Jazz-Dope-and-Fucking-in-The-Streets-Underground-Resistance-Guerrilla-Agitation-Unit of their debut album, *Kick Out the Jams.* To become that PHRRFJDAFITSURGAU, they had to evolve naturally – remember, hard rock didn't exist in 1965. As has been written a billion times, throughout the 60s, Amerikkka was going through a mighty turbulent time: the Martin Luther King assassination, Watts riots, Vietnam, the draft, Leary, etc. With this as a backdrop, the Five, at the will of their insurrectionary manager John Sinclair, took on the mantle of the revolutionary cultural vanguard, as the counterculture's rock 'n' roll assault group, playing throughout the Midwest almost every night, and under constant police harassment. By the time of the recording of KOTJ in October 1968, the MC5 and Sinclair were crippled by legal busts. A British band in the twenty-first century would have to kill a policeman to achieve the notoriety the Five had to tragically live with. And tragedy it was: after that first album, they were fucked: *Kick Out the Jams* is an incendiary device. Actually, it's an incendiary document. Strike that, it's a document that feels like it was once incendiary. Because, brothers and sisters, we all know that by the end of 1968 the 'revolution', which had looked like it might be about to become a reality,

are damned well given (and it will most probably be given to them by a major record label) – I have to concede that if this is the way the pendulum is swinging then Black Box

---

was never going to happen. And as much as *Kick Out the Jams* had sounded like it was kicking down the door that led to a scorched-earth future, there was really nowhere left to go but back. Thus ended phase one of the MC5's artistic life. In the twenty-first century artistic phases have been replaced by career trajectories.

Back in the USA, the second album, from 1970, saw the band enter their retro art phase, casually maligned at the time and a poor seller. Weirdly, the super-taut power pop Little Richard and Chuck Berry covers of *Back in the USA* actually were the future; that future being London in 1976 (for a British band to achieve this MC5 hybrid status they would presumably have to put out a second album's worth of oddly produced Smiths covers). The MC5 had come to a sad realisation, one that the Clash would never fully understand: they were just a rock 'n' roll band. For the twenty-first-century chancer, the knowledge that they are just a rock 'n' roll band isn't so much a realisation as a grim reality from birth. By the time of their third and best album, *High Time*, The Five were on a major downer; shootings at Kent State, Nixon's Amerikkka, and their own failure to, y'know, kick out the jams muthafucka. *High Time*, with its knowing front cover of a busted clock, is an album of high realisation inseparable from the era it was made in, yet at times capable of predicting the grim future. 'Vietnam, what a sexy war,' screams lead singer Rob Tyner on 'Over and Over', and this in 1971, eight years before *Apocalypse Now!* Sheez. It didn't matter, the revolution, cultural and political, was in tatters; the Five became the MC2 and finally called it a day in 1975. Of course, the punk assizes belatedly restored the band's er, ramalamfafafa, and by the early 2000s even silly fashionistas were wearing T-shirts bearing the name of a group whose music they had not heard. This was followed by the inevitable reformation of surviving members and the even more crushingly depressing collaborations with Primal Scream. In our age of no imagination, no moderately successful group will ever split up for longer than six months, and Primal Scream themselves will never

Recorder are gonna be scuppered. When those men in the gorilla suits were briefly all the rage a year or so ago, the supercharged irony of BBR's new album made a kind of sense, but now with all this talk of 'MC5/New York Dolls hybrids' our record sounds adrift on the salty sea of arch glibness. We three, plus manager, sit around the record company meeting table in the impressive One Little Indian office in South London – paid for out of Björk millions – and go through the motions. John and Sarah seem to be enjoying themselves, discussing ideas for album artwork and pondering which track we should release as a single. I'm not enjoying myself, because I am tired of the business of rock 'n' roll and because I know that we are irredeemably fucked.

Whilst the Black Box Recorder album has spent the last year feeling very lonely, sat on a shelf in a receiver's office, the *Christie Malry* film has also not had an easy time of it. Initial private screenings were well received and the prognosis was good, but since then there has been the small matter of September 2001, and *you know what* in New York. Just over a year later in October 2002 is no time to be trying to sell a film about terrorism. This is the hard bit, selling the fucking movie; it is even harder, when your movie ends, as does *Christie Malry*, with your protagonist poisoning 20,000 Londoners. Back in 2000, this celluloid genocide

---

split up, they will always be on hand to put a reassuring arm around the bloated corpse of a legend, ushering them through a lucrative yet humiliating dance of death. Just don't get me started on the New York Dolls.

just seemed like the logical fictitious denouement to a film about a deranged avenging angel, but in the heightened state of paranoia of the post Twin Towers world, it seems less far-fetched. The upshot of all this is that no distributors will go near *Christie Malry's Own Double-Entry*. If we can't get it 'out there', then we are going to be stuck with a very expensive home movie on our hands. Go directly to jail, do not pass go, do not recoup production costs.

So, in November 2002, I sit eating not very nice food in my hundred-pound seat at the Grosvenor House hotel. The fucking Grosvenor House. I've been here before. Happy memories of my own once appalling behaviour flash through my head, and for a few moments I feel once again like a man about to face a firing squad. But this time I know it's all going to be OK, because this time it ain't the Mercury Music Prize, it's the British Independent Film Awards, and I've been nominated in the best soundtrack category for *Christie Malry's Own Double-Entry*, and apart from the odd feeling of déjà vu I'm pretty relaxed, I know I'm safe. I know for a fact that there is more chance of Ian Brady becoming a Blue Peter presenter than me winning this frigging gong.

It's been a good summer. *Christie Malry* has been given a small 'guerrilla' release at a handful of far-flung sympathetic independent cinemas. Every so often I turn up after the actor and director Q & A sessions and strum away a few songs from the soundtrack. I am having a fucking blast, far out in the country and away from the blasted music industry.

A man I do not know has just given me the signal that for some reason he would like me to follow him to the toilets of the Grosvenor House. He wants to share his cocaine with me. Beats me. Anyway, I decline the offer, as the announcement for best soundtrack is about to be made. Dave Pearce. Hahaha, Dave Pearce, some fucking all-purpose Radio 1 DJ who has cobbled together a bunch of all-purpose dance tracks for the soundtrack of an all-purpose Brit flick about clubbing, scoops the bauble. The last time I was on the business end of losing an award was nine years ago at the Mercury Music Prize. Then our table was jammed right up close to the stage next to the eventual winner's table. I thought I was in with a shot. This time I know that the game is up the instant that I am shown to my seat: if I were any nearer the cloakroom I'd be handing out tickets.

The group/manager/record company interface drags indeterminably on. Strategies are tossed around the table, clichés are trotted out, and false horizons are spotted. A single is chosen: 'These Are the Things', my main contribution to the ditty amounts to little more than a Eurodisco chorus that I've copped wholesale from another lame-oid Eurodisco smash. I realise that my effect on this song is entirely negative: if the damned tune ever gets played on the radio, then thanks to me we'll surely be sued for plagiarism.[43] The record and its references suck dead dogs, but it doesn't matter. There are more insurmountable objects in

[43] Luckily 'These Are the Things' is avoided almost entirely by the nation's radio DJs. This follow-up single to 'The Facts of Life' achieves a chart high of number 103. 'I didn't know that it was physically possible for a single to sell so few copies,' quoth John Moore.

flight path BBR. John and Sarah have reached the no-longer-wearing-wedding-rings point in their rock 'n' roll marriage – if only they had bothered to read up on the wisdom of Dr Karl Wilkie. We have a five-album record deal with One Little Indian. It ain't worth the paper it's written on. We are fucked. Irredeemably.

23

'. . . Ze free jazz/hard rock interface'

December 2002. A train journey to the south-west of England. Post Everything. Spawn of Pop Idol *TV show*, Popstars – The Rivals *(second series) gives us two new singing groups: One True Voice and Girls Aloud. The latter bag the Christmas number one with 'Sound of the Underground', an abusive marriage of Dick Dale guitars and crap 80s Po-Mos' Westworld. At the time of writing the hosts have been far too polite, allowing Girls Aloud to long outstay their welcome. On 22 December Joe Strummer dies at home of a heart attack aged 50. North Korea expels UN weapons inspectors and announces plans to reactivate a dormant nuclear fuel processing laboratory. We live in hope.*

It's a preposterous notion, surely doomed from the off, but if I narrow my eyes and look towards the horizon I'm pretty sure I can see the tiniest chink of light. I've been thinking about the idea for a musical on and off for a few years now.

There's everything to lose and the odds are stacked high against me, but I have to follow my compulsion. I should really be giving the BBR situation my full attention, but I can't, my eye drifts helplessly off the ball whenever *Passionoia* business looms. Besides, I know that John Moore and Sarah Nixey are as preoccupied with their own 'solo' projects as I am. When we were thrashing out the One Little Indian deal it felt almost as if Black Box Recorder was just a Trojan horse stuffed full of solo albums, and of course that's something else I should be taking care of, but my heart and mind are lost to the giddy idea of this musical . . . and it won't just be some underachieving two-hander to be performed above a pub in Crouch End. Nope, this one is gonna be the full set. A huge fuck-off Panzer division of a muthafuckin epic. A musical based on the life of Nicholas van Hoogstraten.

I need to get away for a few days, to prepare my grand entrance into the world of 'musical theatre', i.e. start writing. I have received an invitation from my old friends Robert and Brenda Allen to come and stay at their new cottage in Devon. Brenda won't be around as she is off in California, busy with her empire of karate schools for kids. I figure that this will be the perfect opportunity to get some work done – away from London and the constant committee meeting in process that is BBR's album. So in December 2002 I take a few days out on my own and head off towards Devon, where I will stay with Robert Allen. Plotting and planning.

I catch the 4.22 train from London Paddington to Exeter, from where I will make my way to Barnstaple, and then on to my final destination, the Allens' cottage, deep in the

Devon countryside. There's only one way to travel: light and well. Limit your luxuries but make sure they really are luxuries – and pay through the nose for your transit. I hand my first-class ticket to the inspector and make my way to the furthest first-class carriage. I walk through the aisle relieved to find the train and most of its cabins deserted. It's late afternoon in the dead of winter, outside it's cold and dark – the way I like it. I sit down in my seat in the empty compartment and rummage through my bag of belongings: a few extra clothes, a microcassette dictaphone, and the small bottle of laudanum that was given as a wedding present two years ago. I wonder if laudanum has a best-before date.

Apparently laudanum does not have a best-before date, but I take an extra drop to make sure. Just before the train engine grinds into operation, there's a kerfuffle at the other end of the corridor. Football fans, oh Christ, I think to myself. Then the slamming of doors and the reassuring sound of wild yob-call floating away from the departing train back at the station. I lean back in my seat. Relieved. Ideas for the musical drift across my mind. *Do any narcotics have a sell-by date*? I wonder. I start to envisage a chorus line of dandified dwarfs singing a haunting refrain just as a familiar voice snaps me out of my reverie.

'I'm appearing on *Top of the Pops* later this week.' Oh God, The Cellist is leaning against the sliding door of my first-class compartment, and he's intent on giving me an update.

'I'm miming cello, keyboards, and the maracas with Richard Ashcroft,' continues the professional musician in his carefully preserved northern accent. I don't mind The Cellist's gentle goading – besides, I got him the gig with Ashcroft – the thing I really want to say to The Cellist is 'Why are you wearing a green all-in-one body stocking?' but when I open my mouth nothing comes out. It makes no difference, The Cellist is on a roll.

'. . . and then I'm going on a world tour with Talvin Singh,' blusters one of rock's least important journeymen, 'and I'm using all your equipment. It's great to be finally working with some professional musicians. My success must make you really bitter,' continues the all-purpose hired hand hopefully. I'm quite pleased my mouth doesn't work. This is The Cellist's big speech – it is his moment, and who am I to deny him. 'Well, I can't stand around here talking to lazy losers like yourself, I've got a tiny empire to build. Oh, and remember to give me a nice string-arranging credit on *Das Capital* when it comes out, speak to my people about it.' And with that he's off, the green Lycra body stocking making an unfortunate creaking sound as the session man skips off down the train corridor – back into punter class where he belongs. My mouth doesn't work but my legs still do, so I stand up and watch salary boy disappearing out of view. I can just about make out the notice pinned to his back:

The Cellist
Professional Musician
For All Your Musical Requirements.

I remind myself that when I get out of this reverie I must sack The Cellist for ever. Just as I am about to slouch back down, a terrible blood-curdling cry comes from mid-air.

'Share your drugs with me now,' shrieks Sam the Bad Cat as he springs out of an overhead luggage rack and whizzes past my left shoulder. 'Weooow,' says Sam, landing unsteadily on the luxuriant arm of a first-class South Western Railways seat.

'I've been expecting you,' I say to Sam, as I prepare a little laudanum for the junk-crazed tabby. 'What gives, Kitty-o?' I enquire. For some reason the presence of Sam the Bad Cat always makes me speak in a ridiculous retro-hipster slang, but I suppose I should at least be grateful that I can now move my mouth.

'It's nice to see you too,' says Sam sarcastically, 'and what gives, daddy-o, is that there is a hip-hop crew aboard this train bound for Devon and they are looking for you.'

'Wise me up, four paws,' I shoot back to the grimacing pussy cat, my hep talk getting more excruciating by the second.

'Well,' says Sam, 'I met Biggie Smalls and Bruce Lee on the astral plane and I played them your *Oliver Twist Manifesto* album, I thought that Notorious B.I.G. would like it . . .'

'And did they?' I ask eagerly, quite keen on approval from the other side.

'No, they didn't like your album,' says the Bad Cat. 'Biggie said it was like when Paul Simon recorded *Graceland* and stole the native African music. Except in your case it's obviously on a much smaller scale. Anyway, they're working their way through the train looking for you and they want to claim back their music. Oh and Tupac's come along for the ride, him and Biggie have made up in death. Have you got any more laudanum?'

'Ska ska badada yeah,' I reply – in scat.

'I think we should hide,' says Sam the opiate-fixated Bad Cat, licking a druggy paw.

In death, Notorious B.I.G. has not lost weight, I note, as the South Western Railways seat that I am hiding beneath buckles under the enormous dead rapper's girth. Biggie, Tupac Shakur, and Bruce Lee are taking a snack break. Looking for whitey is hungry work for these stiffs. I hear a buffet trolley rattle to a halt outside our compartment.

'Yo, dawg, you got any them Bourbon biscuits?' drawls B.I.G. to the trolley dolly man.

At my eye level on the floor of the carriage I can see a pair of 'box fresh' trainers. Man, hip-hop style is fucking retarded, I note, as the voice that owns the trainers starts chuckling.

'Bo-bon,' laughs Tupac. 'What kinda bitch ass east coast fag biscuit is Bo-bon?' enquires the dead rapper of the other dead rapper sitting opposite.

'Would you prefer a packet of custard creams instead?' asks the West Country-accented trolley dolly man of dead old Tupac.

'Mos def,' says the murdered rapper, to scoffs of disapproval from Smalls, just as Bruce Lee returns from a long and treacherous journey to the buffet carriage.

'There is no green tea aboard South Western train,'

announces the long departed kung fu legend to all in the first-class compartment. Notorious B.I.G. shifts his colossal arse above me and I know I have to act.

'Listen, Tutz,' I whisper to Sam, the last vestiges of hipster speak still with me, 'you've got to get rid of these morons pronto, they're about to reignite their fucking idiotic east coast, west coast rap war over fucking custard creams and Bourbons, and I don't want to get caught in the crossfire . . . do something, Sam the Bad Cat.' With that the mental moggie darts out from beneath the South Western Railways seat and coughs up a disgusting fur ball on Tupac's 'box fresh' trainers.

'Muthafuckin' cocksucker,' yells Shakur at the pussy.

'Hur hur, cat sick funny,' confirms Notorious B.I.G., and with that the two deceased rappers and the deceased martial arts film star lumber out of the first-class compartment in slow pursuit of Sam the speedy Bad Cat.

It's at about this time, as I sit down, once again alone in the train cabin, that I would expect Lawrence, the one-time head honcho of Felt and Denim (and now the leader of Go Kart Mozart), to show up.

'Train approaching Horrabridge Station, all passengers for Horrabridge please disembark here.' I lean into the window just far enough to see the corpse rappers shuffling down the platform. The Cellist lingers a few paces behind, no doubt hoping for some session work, if not in this life then in the next – he is definitely a fucker with a pension plan.

'This train will be continuing on its diversion around

derelict railway stations of the south-west of England,' announces an announcer. 'Next stop Blackdown and Mary Tavy.' The train engine whirrs to a standstill and for a few moments all is quiet. The silence is only broken by the sound of a solitary door slamming shut and a new passenger boarding the first-class carriage. *Man, I still really like drugs*, I marvel, pretty pleased with myself for knowing what's coming next. A man in a tatty leather jacket and a stupid hat appears in the aisle. After what seems like a lifetime spent struggling with the sliding door, the thin man eventually manages to let himself into the first-class compartment.

'Ha, Lawrence, how does it feel to be riding in first class, you motherfucker?' I yell at the frail figure before me.

'I am not Lawrence – leader of Felt, Denim, and of course ze Go Kart Mozart. I am Dr Karl Wilkie of ze Leipzig Institute of ze Cranial Research.' Dr Karl Wilkie offers me his bony hand by way of an introduction. Of course, I know all about the doctor: I have studied his work for years.

Dr Karl Wilkie sits down opposite me, puts his briefcase on his lap, opens it, and gets out some papers and a book, which he places to his side. I recognise the tome immediately as Wilkie's key text: *The Theorem of the Moron*.

'I heard that you became a woman,' I blurt. Even within the relative free-for-all of an opiate reverie this is a stupid thing to say.

'You cannot define me, I define you,' says the doctor sharply, most definitely a man. 'I am working on a case study,' announces Wilkie, fixing me with a stare.

'OK, of whom?' I shoot back.

'I am examining ze variable outcomes,' continues the doctor, 'ze variable outcomes of my studies on *you* – I am on ze vay to visit *you* in Truro, where *you* are recording your third album in a residential studio,' reveals the nutty quack. I see what's going on, it's the old present self meeting younger self shtick (kind of like Roger Moore in the film *The Man Who Haunted Himself* (1975) though hopefully less dreary).

'All right then, Doc, what year is it on your side of the carriage?'

'It eez ze Yule, 1994,' answers Wilkie. *This could be interesting*, I think to myself.

'What happened at the Mercury Music Prize in 1993 in your "variable outcome" world?' I ask.

'You von, of course. Beating ze M. People by ze vun vote.'

'Did it make me a nicer person?'

'For about a week,' says the sawbones of rock. 'Ze second album was still *Scheisse* . . .'

'Woah!' I butt in. 'I have reappraised *Now I'm a Cowboy* and if you separate it from the remedial zeitgeist of the time it holds its own.'

'Zis may be true,' says the loco locum, quizzically, 'but it eez not really for you to say, eez it?'

'Yeah, yeah,' I fire back, noticeably irritated. 'So what happens next?'

'Vell, after several unsuccessful tours supporting ze Lenny Kravitz in Europe, ze Auteurs split, you retire to ze remote Spanish countryside with your – how you say – cock-neez road manager and ze stray dog, it eez here zat you write ze opera dedicated to your Mutter.'

'But that's just the plot of *Stardust*, the classic 1974 movie starring David Essex as Jim Maclaine,' I counter back at the demented old doctor.

'Maybe,' says Wilkie softly, 'but right now you are at ze free jazz/hard rock interface of your life.' Dr Karl Wilkie of the Leipzig Institute of Cranial Research leans forward conspiratorially and hisses, 'Write your musical, otherwise you will be reforming ze Auteurs in 2011 – and zat, mein friend, would not be good.'

'All passengers for Mary Tavy and Blackdown alight here,' crackles a local accent over the tannoy.

'*Auf Wiedersehen*,' bids the doc, struggling once again with the sliding door. One out and one in.

''Ello,' says a Brummie voice.

'Hello, Lawrence.'

I arrive at the Allens' small cottage in the countryside at midnight.

'How was the journey?' asks Robert Allen.

'Uneventful,' I say. 'Have this, it's yours to keep.' I hand Robert the bottle of laudanum.

24

A history of English rottenness during the reign of Queen Elizabeth II

January 2003. How to get a musical put on by the National Theatre using just two scraps of A4 paper.
Post Everything. US plan to invade Iraq. 60,000 troops posted to Persian Gulf. North Korea threatens the United States that it will 'vanish in a sea of fire'. Nasty chemical ricin is found in Manchester and Bournemouth, as nine are arrested in the ongoing 'War on Terror'. There are no longer any surviving members of T. Rex when percussionist Mickey Finn dies. The average house price in the UK is £120,000.

Well, the first thing that will have to change is the title. No one these days likes a long title, and so *A History of English Rottenness during the Reign of Queen Elizabeth II* becomes *Property – A Musical*. The writing at Robert Allen's place in December has gone well and I have a clutch of new songs that will make up the backbone of what will become *Property.* The whole *Christie Malry* experience has been useful in terms of showing me how to get things done outside of the godforsaken music industry. *Ha. You keep on thinking like that, boy*, laughs a griffin of common sense upon my shoulder, before swooping off back into the clouds. I play *Malry* director Paul Tickell some of the demos I have recorded for the proposed musical – Tickell suggests that *Christie Malry* scriptwriter Simon Bent should be on board. Actually I have already drunkenly accosted Simon Bent with my big idea and he's so far rather gamely going along with it, which is ideal as Bent has good chops – having written a number of well-received dramas and had a couple of plays on at the National Theatre, where SB is also a 'writer-in-residence'. Quite what this writer-in-residence scheme may be is unclear; if nothing else it seems to provide shelter and warmth for impoverished playwrights, and as I am beginning to see, all playwrights are impoverished.

January 2003. A municipal building in South London, where I will spend much of the next year, in a partially self-imposed exile from rock 'n' roll, awaiting the verdict upon a couple of tatty sheets of coffee-stained A4 paper that detail the bare bones of a five-act musical I am going to write with Simon Bent.

'It's the first time he's been out of the house since 1971,' Bent whispers in my ear, gesturing towards a particularly decrepit fellow playwright, who is anxiously fumbling with a pile of photocopied pages. Always the sheets of photocopied paper. Looking at the chap's moth-eaten jumper and rats' nest of hair I can't say for sure that Bent is joking. I consider giving the poor fucker a couple of quid but he wouldn't know what to do with it. We are in a world of thick-cut beige cord trousers and mustard brown blazers. The theatre thingys have appalling dress sense. SB and I are in the National Theatre Studio, situated in a 60s utilitarian block, on an unpromising road called The Cut, a few hundred yards from Waterloo Station. The NT studio is where plays get written, pulled apart, rehearsed, interfered with, and – if you're one of the lucky few – put into production at one of the National's three theatres on the South Bank: the Olivier, the Lyttelton, or the Cottesloe. Simon Bent is not having a great time of it; he has recently been on the receiving end of some bad news, having just been told that a play he has been working on for the best part of a year is not yet ready to go into production. Simon, a good ten years older than I am, and frankly not in the best of health, looks like a man who has had the shit kicked out of him by the dragons of good taste. Maybe this isn't the best day to be having a meeting. I am trying hard, really damned hard, not to notice that life in the theatre looks really tough, but then just as the playwright's lot seems insurmountably hopeless, I hear a voice booming away near the fucked 80s drink machines. The voice belongs to actor Michael Gambon, who is happily perched at the communal table of the recreational 'space' (in the theatre, areas and places are referred to as 'spaces'). Though things may not be going well for S. Bent, they are about to perk up for the latent actors and writers assembled at the NT Studio: they are about to be honoured by leading thesp Michael Gambon, who will regale anyone within earshot with his anecdotes of the great and the good; it is, it would seem, an actor's life, a 'wealth of experience' is being shared. I begin to wonder about my own wealth of experience. *Am I perhaps too cynical to live?* I wonder, just as Simon Bent and I are called into an office. We are about to receive the verdict on our tatty coffee-stained pieces of paper.

A nice matriarch sits behind a desk. She is both friendly and brusque. As outward offensives go I can dig her manner. At her side sits a bespectacled little man called Graham. Within seconds of being introduced Graham has told me two things that are entirely irrelevant to any dealings I imagine I may have with him. Graham would like me to know that he is (a) a Marxist, and (b) a homosexual. As conversational opening gambits go it's a helluva non-starter. I take an immediate dislike to Graham. The matriarch senses the discomfort that the little bespectacled lacky has inflicted upon the room and turns her attention towards our tatty pieces of coffee-stained A4 paper that she is now holding between her fingers.

'Now, this is very interesting,' says the matriarch brightly.

Hahahahahaha. Er, ahahahahah. Of course, it's got the lot. A Nick van Hoogstraten-alike in the protagonist Pollard, Brighton racetrack (Graham Greene-lite of course). A Rachman character. Thinly veiled parodies of Jeffrey Archer and Jonathan Aitken. A Maconie-style 70s interlude with binbags rotting in the street during the long hot summer of

1976. Some cobblers about 'Nazi pasts'. Christ, we've even snuck in a sub-plot involving Lord Lucan. What more could anyone want?

Not that much it would seem. The matriarchal lady looks up after having pretended to read our proposal for the first time and says, to both my and Simon's astonishment, 'What do you need from us?'

Caught out in a promising position we manage to stammer some nonsense about 'string sections' and a 'chorus line of around twenty people'. Of course, we really just want to put the damn thing on, and have given no real thought to any practicalities. I'm amazed anyone is taking this seriously at all.

'OK, leave it with us,' says the matriarchal woman, 'we'll get back to you in a week – I'm sure we can come up with something.' Graham shifts uncomfortably in his chair and nods in agreement with his boss – he wanted to make this harder. *Don't worry, Graham, you will get your way.* Simon Bent and I walk out of the NT Studio in stunned happiness, leaving the other playwrights to their self-imposed misery. Simon is temporarily, at least, uncrushed, I am just surprised that someone at the National Theatre appears to be taking our tatty pieces of paper seriously. We do not notice the griffins of doom, who have swooped back up to their perches, just seconds before we walk out of the door.

25

The Grahams

March–July 2003. Writing and 'workshopping' Property *at the National Theatre Studio. Black Box Recorder's third album,* Passionoia, *slips out quietly, almost unnoticed, and in summer 'Das Capital – The Songwriting Genius of Luke Haines and the Auteurs' slips out quietly, almost unnoticed.*

Post Everything. 20 March. Invasion of Iraq begins. A week or so later US troops seize control of Saddam International Airport, renaming it Baghdad International Airport. Nice one. Beagle 2 launched in June. Britain's first unmanned probe is off to Mars. As well as a bunch of academics, some members of Blur and Damien Hirst seem to be involved. Ye gods, it's the Groucho Club in space. Not content with galactic domination Blur give an extra boost to all-points-covered signifier of crap Banksy, when they employ the twenty-first century's worst man to doodle their new album cover. In July, weapons expert Dr David Kelly takes his own life.

The Man Who Used to Be in *EastEnders* for Quite a Long Time is massaging my neck. I'm not a tactile chap. Unless we are exchanging body fluids, or you are a member of my family, then hands off, buster, but these actors, they're so damned touchy. I am grimacing, everywhere I look there is reason to deepen my grimace and further furrow my brow. Butch men do 'stretches' whilst other manly men ostentatiously flaunt their vocal cords – 'a o e o ow e o e u,' they trill. 'Ar ar ar ar arrrr,' they bellow. The Man Who Used to Be in *EastEnders* for Quite a Long Time continues pounding away at my neck.

"You do seem tense," he says, not camp but not quite as tough as his onscreen character. Well, yes. The stretching, the tralala-ing, and the general leotard wearing continue unhindered for far too long, when at last Marxist Graham – Graham Marx – claps his hands. A signal for all the 'warm up' nonsense to stop. For the next two weeks I will turn up at the National Theatre Studio at nine thirty every morning, and I will leave at five o'clock in the afternoon. Myself, Simon Bent, a handful of actors, and Graham Marx are 'workshopping' *Property*. Excuse me, but shouldn't a workshop at the very least have a fucking lathe in it?

A couple of weeks after our initial meeting in January with the nice matriarch at the National Theatre, Simon and I get the call back. When we arrive in the office I am disappointed to find that the nice matriarch has gone – never to return. Perhaps giving *Property* this vague sort of 'green light' was a final act of revenge. The matriarch has been replaced by another Graham: the new Graham sits behind his desk with bespectacled Graham Marx at his side and witters on about Coldplay. People in the theatre don't really like or know anything about music, they only like the theatre. It becomes pretty clear after listening to the two Grahams that people in the theatre don't know anything about anything. Only the theatre, which they know a lot about. As Graham and Graham drone away, I make a silent vow to myself that whatever happens I will remain in blissful ignorance about all things theatrical. Finally, the new Graham – Graham Coldplay – lets Simon and me in on the plan.

'What we'd like to do is "workshop"[44] *Property* for a few weeks, get you together with some actors and a musical director, and see what happens. What do you think?'

I think that I wish I'd brought Manager Charlie to this meeting; other than the fact that we only have a few songs and a couple of tatty pieces of paper describing our as yet unwritten musical, it would seem that we are a few obstacles away from going into full production.

'Workshop it is then,' says Graham Coldplay cheerily. 'See you in the summer.'

Even though I have been preoccupied with my endeavours to bring the life of Nicholas van Hoogstraten to the blue-rinse brigade, it hasn't gone unnoticed that a minor miracle has taken place: in April, Black Box Recorder's *Passionoia* album is finally released – to no small fanfare. In fact it has been released to no fanfare at all. Three-star reviews

[44] Author's inverted commas.

and sixes and sevens all round. The album that was doomed from inception, doomed upon completion, has now completed the holy trinity by being doomed upon its release. John Moore and Sarah Nixey sit forlornly with their ears pressed to the wireless, but alas not a peep from first single, the detested 'These Are the Things'. It's a shame because in the severe light of day *Passionoia* is a good album. Just not right for the times and Black Box Recorder aren't quite dumb enough to bother blowing smoke up anybody's asshole. This is what happens when your attention wanders. We do a whistlestop tour of the UK (six dates) and return to London to the exciting news that our record label, One Little Indian, will not be picking up the option on our contract. We are dropped. On this occasion, it looks unlikely that the Black Box Recorder has survived the crash.

Das Capital – the revenge album against the French regime – is also about to be dusted down. I've kept my head down, and the damn thing is going to see the twinkle of morning. The record will be sneaked out in the dead still air of summer. No fucker will notice it that way: the public, the record company, not even the birds in the trees. There is a final piece of bookkeeping to take care of; it occurs to me that I should 'sack' The Cellist. 'Goodbye,' says The Cellist to me at the end of a series of terse communiqués. 'Goodbye,' I say back.

I spend the early summer waiting for my 'meta hits' album to be released. I idly toy with who we should get in to direct *Property* when 'workshopping' resumes, perhaps *Stewart Home, the artist and writer who sometimes uses long repetitive pornographic sequences for comic conceptual effect and to bolster his word count*, would be good. *Das Capital* is finally released in early July to no fanfare at all. Three-star reviews and sixes and sevens all round.[45] The album that was doomed from inception, doomed upon completion, has now completed the holy trinity by being doomed upon its release. I do not sit forlornly with my ear pressed to the wireless, for alas I know that I will be unlikely to hear a peep from the nation's favourite of my orchestral masterpiece. It's a shame because in the severe light of day *Das Capital* is a good album. Just not right for the times and I'm not dumb enough to bother blowing smoke up anybody's asshole.

Holy mother of god. There's more interference going on here in the NT Studio than at an Irish Catholic orphanage. The main purpose of a 'workshop' it would seem is for The Grahams – and there are now three – to get on my case. I have so far spent a week in a spartan room with a piano trying to write songs – I wasn't banking on sharing this room with Graham Marx, who every morning pulls up a chair

[45] Actually, most of this paragraph isn't strictly true. Obviously I shoehorned Stewart Home's name in there so I could try out his repetition trick, and the album actually receives great reviews across the board, apart from in *Mojo* magazine (see 'Lost mojo' chapter), when the editor rather predictably knocks a star off the reviewer's copy. Not to be outdone by this almost ritualistic pettiness, I make sure that the missing star is reinstated (and I add one more for good measure, giving *Das Capital* the full five-star treatment) when Virgin take out a small advert for *Das Capital* across the three main music monthlies – one of which is *Mojo*.

beside me at the piano and makes 'suggestions' as to how the song I am working on can be improved. Graham Marx has never written a song in his life, in fact he was a telephone engineer until a few years ago. The immediate impulse is obviously to pulverise his stupid head with the grand piano lid, but that would be too easy. Besides, I have to acknowledge that I am playing by different rules down here with the theatre types, so instead of ultra-violence I make sure that any song I am working on is finished before I enter the National Theatre building. This way I can sit down at the joanna and pretend I am working on already completed songs 'taking on board Graham's helpful advice'. It's an old pros' trick, and Graham Marx is not an old pro so my plan works. But fear not, there is more: another Graham has been drafted in. This Graham is the musical director; he looks like Dr Mengele. So after Graham Marx has had a fiddle about with my work, Graham Mengele gets to stick his beak in. Actually Graham Mengele isn't too bad – you see, it's all about chucking them scraps. If Mengele makes ten suggestions I concede on one – the least important – and praise the Graham for his good idea. Of course, Graham Mengele is also an old pro, and knows exactly what I'm up to, but for now he doesn't push.

Finally, after all the Grahams have satiated themselves with a good old fiddle, we have enough material to let some actors loose on it. Whilst I have been undergoing torture sessions from Mengele and Marx, Simon Bent has locked himself away in his 'writer in residence' attic high above the prying eyes of anyone called Graham. He should be so fucking lucky.

The Man Who Used to Be in *EastEnders* for Quite a Long Time furrows his brow and then laughs.

"You two are well mental," he chuckles at Simon and myself, having read the scene he is to star in. The Man Who Used to Be in *EastEnders* for Quite a Long Time has flown in from his home in Portugal to be in our 'workshop'. He could never have guessed it was going to pan out like this: one minute you're sitting in Ian Beale's 'orrible caff, the next you're playing a van Hoogstraten-alike and singing a duet with Lord Lucan just before you murder him. Graham Marx shifts uneasily in his chair. What if The Man Who Used to Be in *EastEnders* for Quite a Long Time is right, and Simon and I are 'well mental'? Graham will never know.

The actors are brought in and the couple of weeks' work starts to come together. The scene we have been working on features our protagonist Guy Pollard (Nicholas van Hoogstraten-alike, played by The Man Who Used to Be in *EastEnders* for Quite a Long Time) and Lord Lucan. Pollard has realised that the disgraced aristo Lucan – on the run after accidentally murdering his children's nanny – is holed up in one of his bedsits. Pollard has confronted Lucan and is now about to murder him. Of course, as this is 'musical theatre' this is all done via song. Hahahahah. What a fucking hoot. The scene is great, everyone breathes a sigh of relief, and the three Grahams (plus an extra battalion of Grahams who have been brought in as a makeshift audience) give us a fulsome round of applause. At the end of the workshop we hop off to the local hostelry.

The two weeks have been a blast. Graham Marx and

Graham Coldplay take Simon and me aside and give us some good news.

'I'd like to take this to Graham Mustard, the big boss upstairs. I think it's just what he's looking for.'

'Mental,' whispers The Man Who Used to Be in *EastEnders* for Quite a Long Time as he passes.

26

The gear and the 'fucking gear'

September–November 2003. Black Box Recorder get 'un-dropped' by their record label and 'celebrate' by going on tour in America. Post Everything. Concorde makes its last flight. Car bombs in Istanbul, and in November George W. Bush makes a state visit to the UK, amidst massive public protests. The Libertines release their first album, Up the Bracket. *Against all odds it's good. Really good. Don't worry, it's all downhill from here as Pete Doherty quickly pursues a new career as a low-level national pest. It's almost admirable. Almost. Suede split up.*

For the first time in 11 years I am without a record label. After the *Das Capital* album has done its 'back catalogue' thing I am well and truly dropped; persona non grata at Virgin Records. Hut Records will be closed down by the idiot French, and David Boyd, the hero of the 90s music biz, will move on. Black Box Recorder have also been dropped, and reside in a tacitly dormant state. I couldn't give a stuff. For now, I have enough money to live on, and I have a musical to write. Then something happens that is unprecedented in all rock 'n' roll lore. Black Box Recorder get 'un-dropped' by their record label.

Tinkle tinkle. Bleep brrrp.

'The record label are saying that they still really love the band,' says Manager Charlie, on the other end of the fucking telephone, 'and when they said they were not going to continue the option, they didn't mean they wanted to drop you.'

'Huh?' I muster.

'They'd like to continue with the contract and they would like Black Box Recorder to record another album . . .'

'So, er, what's the catch?'

'They are only willing to pay you half the advance.'

I put down the receiver and have a very short think. In late 2003, let us be under no illusion, we are in the age of the twilight of the record company advance. If there is one thing I knew way back in the cursed old 1990s, if it walks like an advance, and it smells like a record company advance, and it talks like a record company advance – then it is a goddamn record company advance, and in the age of the twilight of the record company advance, then you'd better just reach out and take it, boy. So we have a little BBR committee meeting – Manager Charlie, me, and The Other Two – and decide that yep, it is an advance, and yes, we will take it. There is also a mini-American tour in November that has been long booked. There is unlikely to be any more *Property* work until the New Year, so, as the body has been dragged out of the water, with new life breathed into its lungs, there may be no harm in going west. The band's last album, *The Facts of Life*, did relatively well in America – give it one last shot. You learn to take what you can from the music industry. American tours, reduced advances. 'S all free money, innit.

My Les Paul Custom guitar, an acoustic guitar, John Moore's Midi guitar (plus spare), our FX pedals, and all of our keyboards have gone missing. We: Moore, Sarah Nixey, and I – Black Box Recorder – stand alone in the reception area of LA's Sunset Marquis Hotel, unadorned by the accoutrements of the modern travelling rock 'n' roll group – our fucking gear. The responsibility for making sure that group arrives at destination of gig with the 'fucking gear' intact is down to one person: the tour manager. In a moment of madness, just prior to boarding a dawn flight from New York to LAX, and shorn of our militaristic American road crew (who have flown on ahead), Sarah and I nominate John Moore to be temporary tour manager. How we smirk amongst ourselves, what a hoot. The power instantaneously goes to Old Moore's head, as he starts barking out orders in a weird, agitated, high-pitched voice, like a slightly dotty auntie in charge of a school trip.

'Luke, Sarah, run and get a couple of trolleys for the equipment,' squawks the despotic temporary tour manager. 'Then when you've done that I'll need everybody's passports.'

Sarah and I stand in silence watching the penny dropping on to the floor in slow-mo. What a fantastic gag: give all the responsibility to the worst possible person, light the touch-paper and see what happens. Old Moore is on a roll, he's been put in charge – and by God is he going to abuse his power. For five long hours we get a mid-air barrage of goading, nagging, petty ordering about, and mini-me Bonapartisms. We have created a monster, and this monster will not let up until we reach our destination.

We breeze through customs at LAX, the temporary tour manager still barking away to no one in particular: 'Passports, passports, chop chop.' Having realised that our joke of promoting the wrong man has backfired, and since the 'wrong man' is not going to shut up until we reach the hotel, we take the obvious course of action: ignore the tour manager. Here we are, just another happy bunch of tourists looking for a cab outside the airport. Don't forget your hand luggage.

A heavily tattooed man in knee-length khaki shorts and an impressive utility belt walks up to me in the reception of the Sunset Marquis Hotel.

'So what happened to the gear, dude?' Tattoos on his forehead rippling slightly with annoyance beneath his base-ball cap, Rik is part of our LA road crew who have flown ahead. In the past I'd had some problems with American crews, but right now as I become more authoritarian, I'm really liking their paramilitary spiel. Man, these fuckers are like a super-fit SAS. Black Box Recorder on the other hand are like the wine-tasting division of a particularly effete branch of the Women's Institute. I give Rik the old nothing-to-do-with-me-it-was-him routine, gesturing at John Moore, whose triumphant yet strange boss man spiel has now evaporated at the sight of Super Rik and been replaced by a more fitting John Le Mesurier air of vagueness. Rik looks at me for a while and says nothing. He doesn't need to, I can read his every thought:

1. You do not take roadie-ing lightly; the job of tour manager is an esoteric discipline that damn fool musicians could never understand.
2. You do not treat the instruments with anything less than the utmost respect. To you the instruments are just the 'fucking gear'. To me they are sacrosanct. The 'fucking gear' has value. You don't.
3. Most importantly, you do not make fucking John Moore tour manager.
4. Why the fuck do you English bands bother? Do you think anyone here gives a fuck about your goddamn faggot teabag music?

Actually, I'm not sure Super Rik consciously endorses clause four – he seems like a well-bred free-thinking boy after all. It's just that deep down I'm sure he's wondering what business John Moore and I have with the business of rock in America.

I breathe in. It's understood, Rik. I furrow my brow, making sure that my thoughts of goodwill commune with

Rik's super-roadie mind. Out of the corner of my eye I can see John Moore sidling into a lift.

'Don't worry, dude, I'm on it,' yells Super Rik as he jumps into a cab bound for the airport, on a mission to rescue the 'fucking gear' before it makes its merry way to Mexico.

You can never turn power and responsibility into a joke: it will only blow up in your own face.

We fly out to New York with a glimmer of hope, the three of us plus a friend of Moore's called Paul the Postman, who claims to be the head of the Peter Cook Appreciation Society. Our useless non-anthem 'These Are the Things' is making surprising (to me at least) progress up the college radio charts and by the time we get into a holding pattern at JFK we have picked up even more alt rock radio ads. America still has a tiny place in its cruel heart for Black Box Recorder.

Apart from that rum incident with the two chaps in the gorilla suits a couple of years ago, America doesn't really do Post Everything 'rock'. Why be self-conscious or ironic when your mother tongue is the very language of rock 'n' roll? BBR are here ostensibly for the CMJ convention – a music biz schmooze mash-up. Pimps get on with pimping and the punters punt. The hot new whores learn how to pick up tricks, and the old tarts gamely put on too much slap. Black Box Recorder are playing, along with a bunch of unreconstructed yank guitar churners, the CMJ opening night party, supporting a recently thawed-out Killing Joke in the 3,000-capacity Webster Hall in Midtown Manhattan. The show is a sound check-less disaster, and the jury is well out as to whether the USA is ever going to take to two men in white suits flanking a prim and waspish lady. Downstairs alt rock legend Bob Mould is playing records in between being humiliated by Paul the Postman. The Postman is very keen on asking the ex-Hüsker Düde the name of his new DJ-ing venture.

'What's it called again?' shouts The Postman into Mould's legendary lughole.

'Bob Mould's Blow Off,' answers Mould, quite factually.

'Sorry, still can't hear you,' counters Paul the Postman.

'Bob. Mould's. Blow. Off,' enunciates the man who influenced Pixies and Nirvana, handing the gleeful postie a business card. Paul the Postman gallops back to me standing at the bar and, with the unadulterated joy of a seven-year-old who's just chanced upon the holy grail of funny, shows me the business card.

'Look. It says "Bob Mould's Blow Off". Do you see?'

I do indeed. The Postman is delirious with joy at his discovery of this lost-in-translation faux pas. You can take the Englishman out of England . . .

Leaving Paul the Postman in New York, incapacitated with mirth, we cross the bridge and head into New Jersey, where 'These Are the Things', the lame-oid bum-boy non-anthem is now a bum-boy anthem. It's still very lame of course, but we have found our audience in New Jersey, where every queen in Hoboken has come to worship at the church of

Black Box Recorder. The gig is fabulous. This, it would seem, is where Black Box Recorder fit in to the American scheme of things. A sea of studded belts, wrist bands, and leather caps bump and grind – Christ, it's fantastic and just like *Cruising* out there. In this parallel universe of New Jersey 'These Are the Bloody Things' is the number one song in Heaven.

LA is gripped in apocalyptic panic. Seasonal late-November forest fires tear through the suburbs and newscasters predict Armageddon. Last night's show at the Irving Plaza was a triumph, though the crowd were noticeably less of a 'These Are the Things' crowd and more of an Anglophile 'Child Psychology' mob. Moore takes his early-doors whiskies and retires to bed. I take late-night whiskies and hit Sunset Strip – the second-least responsible person now upgraded by JM's premature departure to irresponsibility club class. Through some terrible oversight I have been put in charge of the tour float. Come the morning I have vague memories of staggering along the strip – bottle of whisky in one hand, tour float in the other, but it's OK, I know it's gonna be all right because I have Super Rik to guide me. In the bastard sunlight of an LA morning it's a relief to find the 'missing' tour float safe in the (real) tour manager's possession. I find it oddly comforting that at the age of 36 I am still as 'capable' as any rock 'n' roll moron ten years my junior of drunkenly losing a large bundle of cash. The end of the world is always nigh in LA; we race to the airport – which due to the forest fires is threatening to close down. It's imperative that we get a flight home. We haven't been here long, but we really need to go.

I spent the 90s touring too much with people I didn't like. I spent the years after that not touring enough with people I do like. We all have an unspoken suspicion that this may be Black Box Recorder's last tour.[46] It's too late to change anything now. The cabin of the near empty plane fills with the smell of smoke from the fires below. America, of course, remains unconquered, but Hoboken, New Jersey, is ours.

[46] It is, and our last gig for five years.

27

Excess baggage

December 2003–February 2004. Decision reversed again for Black Box Recorder. Property *officially becomes a National Theatre 'concern'.*

Post Everything. Mars probe, Beagle 2, is lost in space. In February BBR's old Top of the Pops *pal Britney Spears gets married in Vegas, and Shoko Asahara, leader of the Japanese Aum cult that launched a gas attack on the Tokyo subway, is sentenced to death.*

On returning from our short jaunt in the US, we really should be at least thinking about how to make the new Black Box Recorder album, the new Black Box Recorder album that none of us, if we are honest (and we are not), wants to make. John Moore has a solo album almost finished, as does Sarah, and I am busy with *Property.* There is also the small matter of the argument that has been snowballing out of control, almost from the minute our plane touched down.

It begins with the tour float, which Super Rik the tour manager had rescued from my drunken hands back in LA. We arrive at Heathrow with a small amount to pay on excess baggage. What with all those extra-size meals, the 'fucking gear' has gained a few pounds in weight over in the USA. We don't have enough cash in the tour float to cover the charge so I pay the excess on my credit card – Black Box Recorder's excess baggage charge comes to a little over $100. I think no more of it.

Over the Christmas and New Year period the National Theatre Grahams have had a little conflab and have waved our coffee-stained scraps of A4 paper under Graham Mustard's sniffy boss man nose. Herr Mustard has also been sending out his winged monkeys to report back to him on the progress of our 'workshop' sessions. Monkey see good things, and in January 2004 Simon Bent and I are commissioned to write *Property*. For the next few months we go into the National Theatre Studio every day at nine o'clock and leave at five o'clock. Just a coupla regular schmucko commuters punching the fucking clock. Although we have been commissioned to write *Property*, this does not necessarily mean that *Property* will go into production. So begin several months of doublespeak. Ah, what the fuck, it's going to be a blast.

I phone Manager Charlie to tell him the good news about the musical.

'. . . Oh, and can you ask the record label to reimburse me that $100 that I paid out on my credit card for excess baggage?' Manager Charlie assures me that he will speak to them. I put the phone down and time is suspended for two weeks.

'Did you ask the record company about that $100?' I say to Charlie, two weeks later, resuming our conversation, having not moved.

'Erm, yes I did,' says Charlie. Ten seconds' silence. 'They said they're not going to pay you the money.' Thirty seconds' silence.

'Ask them again then. They owe me $100. It's not much. Look, I don't even care if they never actually get round to paying me the $100, I'd just like them to acknowledge that in principle *they owe me* the $100 I paid for excess baggage,' I say with remarkable composure. I put the phone down and stand suspended in time for three weeks waiting for the phone to ring. Brrrp Brrrp. It's the fucking phone.

'I've asked them again for the $100,' begins Manager Charlie.

'And?' I interrupt, already seething.

'They say that you can work it off. If you record a Black Box Recorder EP, they will pay you the $100, which they see as money *you owe them*.' Silence for 58 seconds, as the words 'If you record a Black Box Recorder EP, they will pay you the $100' swirl around in my head.

'So, the budget for the US tour is all agreed in advance,' I begin coolly. 'And because we go over the budget – that had all been agreed beforehand – with a nebulous $100 excess baggage fine, that $100 becomes money I owe to them?' I continue.

'That is how they see it,' confirms Manager Charlie.

'So isn't asking Black Box Recorder to record an EP, which the record label will then pay me $100 for – money they claim I owe them – tantamount to an admission that they actually owe me $100?' I rationalise. Very long silence.

'Tell 'em to fuck off,' I say to Manager Charlie before slamming down the phone.

Five minutes later Manager Charlie calls back. Having told the record company to fuck off.

'They've had enough. You're dropped again.' I feel bad for John and Sarah, but it turns out that they don't feel bad at all. No one really wanted to make the new album anyway. The record company don't even ask for the advance they've already paid us back. Thank you, gents, it's a pleasure doing business with you. I'm a man who's lost $100 but found £20,000. Record advances – 'sall free money, innit?

28

Mental

July 2004. A soap star goes doolally.
Post Everything. Saddam Hussein put on trial. The Butler Review criticises the UK government for using 'unreliable evidence' in relation to weapons of mass destruction. David Bowie suffers a minor heart attack.

'You two are well mental.' The parting words of The Man Who Used to Be in *EastEnders* for Quite a Long Time, just over a year ago, prior to jumping on a plane back to the Costa Del Soap. In the space of 14 months a man can change his mind about things. The cogs that power the thespian bonce are a precision piece of apparatus, so in the present circumstances we can only say in delayed reply to The Man Who Used to Be in *EastEnders* for Quite a Long Time, 'No, sir. It is you who is behaving in a rum old way.' There are dark and likely wildly exaggerated rumours going around the National Theatre Studio, that he has been studying The Stanislavski System, wanting to become 'a serious actor', whisperings of bad behaviour on sets, of being sacked from a TV drama for calling a child actor a 'cunt' and making them cry (obviously this endears him to me quite a lot). Our cheery geezerish leading man who loved Simon, me, and *Property* so much when we were last all together back in March 2003 has returned to the fold, a somewhat burdened lost sheep, for what will turn out to be our last 'workshop', not quite so cheery and geezerish and most definitely not quite so in love with Simon, me, or *Property*. Perhaps he has had too much time rattling around his Portuguese pile, watching *Persona*, or *Performance*, dressed only in his underpants. Maybe he has been immersed in the writings of Luis Borges, or just rattling around in his mansion like Jim Maclaine in *Stardust*.[47] It's one helluva midlife crisis, that's for sure, and we are now in the company of a very different and very frightening Man Who Used to Be in *EastEnders* for Quite a Long Time. There is something rotten on the Costa Del Soap.

Throughout the spring and early summer, Simon and I work tirelessly on *Property* in the cramped rehearsal rooms of the NT Studio. We are paid approximately £150 per week and we don't pull a single sickie. It's a great way to write – apart from the endless interference by the committee of Grahams who are swarming all over us. Why didn't I write as prolifically as this

[47] Final mention of David Essex.

when I was being paid vast publishing advances by major record labels? Beats me. Musicals are either a fool's or a madman's folly – they can take years to write, but by June 2004 we have a good first draft of *Property*. Comes the hour, comes the man. It is now time to go and see Graham Mustard.

Graham Mustard runs the joint. A dead-eyed dilettante who surrounds himself with a pointless committee of yes men. An artless autocrat who preaches creativity but sings from the hymnbook of business. Mustard is feared by all who creep through the corridors of the National Theatre. He is known for two things: his lack of personality and his lack of a sense of humour. Graham Mustard has turned both of these unappealing traits entirely to his advantage. Of course, having a sense of humour is overrated but everyone on earth has or at least *thinks* they have a sense of humour. Even Hitler had a go at cracking the odd gag.[48] Not so Graham Mustard. This fucker has not one joke cell in his body. Less laughs than a yearly subscription to *Mojo* magazine. The best thing about all of this is that Mustard's absence of funny bone does not concern him one jot. He is Yul Brynner's deadly assassin robot in *Westworld*, dressed in a horrid jaundice-coloured blazer. Graham Mustard is one heck of a

[48] Hitler's favourite joke: according to *The Last Witness*, a book by Rochus Misch – a telephonist in Hitler's Berlin bunker during April 1945, the butt of the Führer's 'jokes' was Luftwaffe commander-in-chief Hermann Goering. Goering was a keen self-awarder of medals. Hitler recounted how Mrs G. found her husband waving a baton over his underwear in the bedroom and asked him what he was doing. The Führer liked to crack that Goering replied, 'I am promoting my underpants to overpants.'

cold fish. Graham Marx, Graham Coldplay, and Mustard's right-hand lady, a fembot called Graham Braun, lead Simon and me up the stairs to the Eagle's Nest high up in the belfry of the South Bank complex overlooking the Thames. We are shown into a large yet oddly claustrophobic conference room with six chairs around a table. The five of us sit down, leaving one empty chair at the head of the table. Everything in the room is painted a different shade of yellow, this is the lair of either a mad genius or a total moron. None of us dare speak – in the war rooms of the National Theatre, the walls have ears. I have been so preoccupied with the stifling hothouse atmosphere of my bizarre surroundings that I have not noticed that the sixth chair, at the head of the table, is now occupied. Graham Mustard shifts some photocopied papers around in his cold hands then looks up, at no one in particular. Eye contact as you may have guessed is not one of Graham Mustard's strong points.

'Before zis meeting commences, I have to change my jacket,' announces Mustard to the room. He stands up and takes off his nicotine-coloured sports jacket and hands it to an underling, who in turn hands her boss an expensive beige cardigan for him to change into. He still looks like shit.

'*Schnell, schnell!*' screams Graham Mustard at the underling, who scuttles back to her mouse hole at the sound of her leader's raised – yet strangely lacking in authority – voice.

'Zat is better,' says Mustard, now blending in with the décor and comfortable in his new knitwear. 'I have read zis script and it is most promising,' continues the Führer, not exactly sounding enthusiastic and still utterly unable to make eye contact with Simon or myself. 'You will do vun more verkshop, and zen you vill perform ze whole piece in its entirety for my benefit. I will zen, and only zen, make my decision as to if and ven ze piece goes into production.' At this, Graham Mustard's right-hand fembot Graham Braun leaps up from her chair and starts applauding. On cue, Grahams Marx and Coldplay begin bowing their heads. Simon Bent and I turn and look at each other, as Graham Mustard's eyes close and his body goes into automatic shut-down. A shiver runs down my spine. By National Theatre standards, and considering we are now in a shadowy world where doublespeak is the language of choice, then this has been a very good meeting.

Simon Bent and I put in a couple more weeks' work on our *Property* script, buffing and polishing. By July we are ready to put the monster through its paces in a final 'work-shop' at the National Theatre Studio. Still not a lathe in sight, though there are of course plenty of tools. But the biggest tool seems to have gone missing. The Man Who Used to Be in *EastEnders* for Quite a Long Time has gone AWOL. Straight off the plane from the Costa Del Soap and straight into the nearest old man's pub right outside Waterloo Station, the nutty bunker, from where he will send his hapless emis-saries with his latest loony despatches, the first of which is that he 'will not be singing today' or at any time in the near future. If you are the leading man in a musical this is a tough one to pull off. Grahams Marx and Coldplay are going spare, our director, erm, Graham Director, is mightily pissed off, and the rest of the cast are getting unnerved. Presumably when your leading man goes off on one this is the equivalent of the captain of the football team saying, 'I don't really fancy this I'd much rather have been a cricketer' just before kick-off. It ain't that good for morale. What this fruit loop soap star hasn't accounted for is that when it comes to having a bit of a think in the pub, I too have a 'wealth of experience to draw upon', as they say in the theatre. I decide that the best thing to do is wait it out. When a man wants to have an alehouse melt-down, the worst thing you can do is stand in his way.

The morning comes and goes in a slow-moving war of attrition. The Man Who Used to Be in *EastEnders* for Quite a Long Time has become *The man who's been in the pub quite a long time*. Simon and I, Grahams, and the cast sit around in the large aircraft hangar studio twiddling our thumbs, wasting time and wasting money. There is plenty of opportunity for shoulder massaging. Finally at lunchtime we receive word from the boozer. *The man who's been in the pub for quite a long time* has decided that he is prepared to join us on one condition: that he will only 'act' whilst sitting cross-legged on the floor. On no account will acting be done 'standing up'. Man, I thought that pop stars were arseholes. Graham Director has had enough of this horse shit and quite impressively storms off to the pub to have it out with our soapy, er, maverick. The question is – are we now in a two men overboard to the boozer situation?

Yes. Graham Director strides purposefully into the National Theatre Studio, and trailing behind him like a sulky teenager is *the man who's been in the pub quite a long time disappointingly sober, considering the hours he's put in*. Simon and I take our seats around the table in the middle of the large studio with the other twelve actors. It is quite difficult to come to an agreement with someone who doesn't know what they want. It's even harder when you think you know what they want but you cannot give it to them. It's becoming clear that what The Man Who Used to Be in *EastEnders* for Quite a Long Time wants is *to not be* The Man Who Used to Be in *EastEnders* for Quite a Long Time. It's even harder to not be The Man Who Used to Be in *EastEnders* for Quite a Long Time when there is always someone waving at you wherever you go, for that very reason, because you are The Fucking Man Who Used to Be in *EastEnders* for Quite a Long Time. Fame, it would seem, in a no-shit-Sherlock scenario, can drive you round the fucking bend. The other thing our leading man wants – though he hasn't quite worked it out for himself yet – is to not be in our musical. Of course, it would now be best if The Man Who Used to Be in *EastEnders* for Quite a Long Time just hopped on board a plane back to the Costa Del Soap. That would be best. But we are playing by theatre rules, where transparency is replaced by obfuscation and plain talk is rejected in favour of doublespeak, so during the lengthy pub sojourn, it transpires, Graham Director has brokered a rather pointless compromise with The Man Who Used to Be in *EastEnders* for Quite a Long Time. There will be no acting as such – sitting on the floor or otherwise – but our star is (at a stretch) prepared to sit around the table with the other actors and take part in a reading of the final script of *Property*.

It's now four o'clock in the afternoon; we should have been doing this 'reading' at nine o' clock in the morning. The demented soap star grumpily plonks himself into a plastic chair; he has of course worked himself up into a proper foul mood. The other actors and Grahams look on nervously. It's going to be an unpleasant afternoon.

'Did you ask him about the singing?' I whisper to Graham Director.

We almost make it . . . to the bottom of page one of the script, that is, before The Man Who Used to Be in *EastEnders* for Quite a Long Time, who is unpleasantly slouched like a truculent adolescent (a bad look when you're on the wrong side of 40), begins aggressively taking issue with the gentle-natured Simon Bent over the script. Funny that these things never seemed to bother him on *EastEnders*. An actor bravely tries to remonstrate with the soap rebel without an IQ and gets a 'fuck you' for his trouble. This is followed by the sound of a collective sharp intake of breath from the assembled cast around the table. I've done this petulant act many times in the past and, grimly fascinating as it is to observe, I can see that The Man Who Used to Be in *EastEnders* for Quite a Long Time is reaching the wounded buffalo death rattle part of his performance – and it is a performance. I decide to give him some help.

'How about we do a bit of singing instead then . . .' I offer. The Man Who Used to Be in *EastEnders* for Quite a Long Time turns slowly to me, neck veins bulging, face purple with rage, and leans across the table until he is two inches from my face, and roars out each word:

'Shut. The. Fuck. Up.'

That's it, job done. The turn cannot tell the writer to 'Shut. The. Fuck. Up.' I outrank him. The beast has been put out of its misery. Graham Director calls a halt to the farrago and within minutes The Man Who Used to Be in *EastEnders* for Quite a Long Time is heading off back into the perpetual sunset of the Costa Del Soap, where presumably he can walk through the olive groves unbothered by middle-aged women whispering, 'Ooh is it 'im?' behind his back. Weirdly, The Man Who Used to Be in *EastEnders* for Quite a Long Time passes on a message before he flies home, saying how much he likes Simon and me, and how he loves our musical. What a fucking dunce.

'Now, who wants to take the lead part in a musical?'

A sea of hands goes up.

29

'I've met the man in the street – and he's a cunt'

October–November 2004. Writing the Off My Rocker at the Art School Bop *album and performing a musical. Preparing to make a plate of scrambled eggs.*
Post Everything. Yasser Arafat dies, as does 'Crazy Horse' Emlyn Hughes and chimney exploder Fred Dibnah. George W. Bush wins second term in office.

I have played no gigs this year. I have had no records released, and I have recorded no songs. Black Box Recorder are on an indefinite hiatus, so for the first time in 17 years I am no longer a member of an unpopular music group. I have long since stopped reading the music press or music monthly magazines, I do not listen to the radio, and I know nothing about new groups or even the current machinations within the music industry. I am out of the loop and I like it. Happy and ignorant. At almost 37 years old my lack of rock 'n' roll presence seems quietly dignified. Quietly dignified but for the fact that I've gone and written a fucking musical. I have spent 18 months working on this damned thing, this beast, and in less than one month's time we may learn its fate. On reflection, it occurs to me that I may have put all my eggs in one basket. The only two people who truly understand this musical are – Simon Bent and myself. A lot of the time has been spent working in solitude: me in an annex of the National Theatre Studio hammering away amateurishly at the joanna, Bent hiding upstairs immersed in the chaos of his reams of photocopied paper; a couple of times a week we converge and meld our work together. To the wider 'music world' I am now invisible. I decide that I will use the small amount of time before we prepare for our performance of *Property* by capitalising on the work rate of the musical and to see if I can write enough songs for an album. A back-up plan of sorts. I give myself a week.

Songs come quick and clean, I hide away up in the highest practice rooms of the National Theatre Studio, not playing the piano too loud in case anyone listens too closely. It would not be good if these Guardians of the Play realise that what I'm up to doesn't have a fuck of a lot to do with 'musical theatre'. The first ditty I pluck out of the air, 'Leeds United', is not dissimilar to 'The Rubettes' from some five years ago, the germ of a Black Box Recorder song, for our unwritten and barely thought-about 'fourth' album. It starts as a 'love' song or mundane conversation at least, between Peter and Sonia Sutcliffe – lately I've been reading Gordon Burn's

Ripper book, *Somebody's Son, Somebody's Husband*. It soon becomes clear that this iron fist will never fit the Black Box Recorder velvet glove, the impetus changes, and the song becomes about Yorkshire at the end of the 70s – via David Peace's *Red Riding Quartet*[49] – and the last few years of the Ripper case. There are many Sutcliffe myths: Leeds United fans chanting, 'Ripper 13, police nil' after the body of the thirteenth victim was discovered; Sutcliffe whiling away his spare time in a decrepit waxwork museum, and that during the long, botched investigation Jimmy Savile was at one point interviewed by the West Yorkshire police. 'Leeds United' is just a folk song with car boot sale orthodox glam rock drums.

The idea of knocking out a folk-glam record begins to take root. Besides, as I listen to no current music I only have what is indelibly stamped upon my ignorant mind:[50] glitter rock. 'Bad Reputation' is a hymn to betrayal, betrayal

[49] When 'Leeds United' is released on November 2006, there is an assumption made that the song is a kind of counterpoint to David Peace's *Damned United* bestseller. It is not. 'Leeds United' is set at the end of the 70s. Peace's book is set in 1974. Also, although there are football references within the song, 'Leeds United' refers to the people of Leeds being united, in fear, hatred, and paranoia, against the ever present spectre of the Yorkshire Ripper.

[50] I am so lacking in any contemporary musical knowledge at this point that I am unaware of the art rock/post-rock revival that is going on. The kids, it would seem, have been lapping up their granddads' Gang of Four albums. Come in, sir, we have so been expecting you. When the song 'Off My Rocker at the Art School Bop' is released in 2006, it is seen as cocking a snook at the whole art rock scene. Once again, not so; it is merely a fond remembrance of being a wallflower at the art college disco.

of the happy memories of a 70s childhood sat in front of *Top of the Pops* by the greatest light entertainment boogieman of the Post Everything age: Gary Glitter.[51] God help those poor saps in the Glitter Band, God help us all – I mean, what hope is there for any of us when we've been let down so, so very badly by the one that no one calls 'The Leader' any more. Two more songs, 'All the English Devils' and 'Freddie Mills Is Dead',[52] are lifted from the pages of the late David Seabrook's psycho-geographical journey through Kent, *All the Devils Are Here*. At the end of the week I have amassed enough material for an album. I file away the songs and hope I won't need them too soon.

This is what it has all been for. Judgement day is upon us. The drunken idea sketched out on two pieces of coffee-stained A4 paper has led us here, to a sound-stage-sized studio in the bowels of the National Theatre Studio on a warm and sunny Thursday in early November: 12 actors, 4 musicians, a choreographer (a fucking choreographer), an

[51] Gary Glitter was merely a ghost on his own records. The true genius of that run of ground-breaking hit singles was producer and songwriter Mike Leander.

[52] Freddie Mills was crowned the light heavyweight champion of the world in 1948. Following his death by gunshot – ruled as suicide by the police – in July 1965, Mills became the subject of rumours: that he was bisexual and had an affair with cabaret singer Michael Holliday, and that he was murdered by the Kray Twins. One of the more persistent whispers after his death linked Freddie Mills to the murder of eight prostitutes between 1959 and 1965 – the so-called Jack the Stripper murders remain unsolved.

MD (musical director), Graham Director, Simon Bent, me, and a nice lady who 'prompts' the actors if they forget a line – all waiting in excitable anticipation. We've got one shot at it – and this is it.

I am suited and booted – 36-hole Doc Martens, not seen too often around these parts but ideal for kicking namby-pamby 'musical theatre' butt. The path here has been littered with incendiary devices – a constant carping from the Greek chorus of the ever-present committee; the willingness of those with seemingly very little experience to pipe up and tell us where we are going wrong; the willingness of those with a 'wealth of experience' to pipe up and tell us where we are going wrong; the meetings . . . the endless bloody meetings. Graham Marx doing his Columbo shtick at the end of a meeting, as we are about to leave the room:

'There is just one thing that is troubling me . . .' Every. Single. Time.

The total and stupefying lack of any sense of humour, the irritation that these people, some of whom may actually be quite bright, seemingly have no knowledge of a world outside the theatre. Graham Coldplay and his tokenistic liking of, well, Coldplay, as a strategic signifier to somehow demonstrate that he's not just a fusty old woman, and that he really does like a bit of rock music. The niggling references in contemporary plays to the Clash by middle-aged playwrights. The plays about Iraq. The plays about 'young people going to raves'. In 2004. The plays about teenage gangs. The 'worried liberal' plays in the style of urban realism all about the 'state of modern Britain'. (Why would any fucker cough up fifty sovs to watch this of an evening when you can stand in your local Costcutter and get it for free? And not worry. Cheez.) So, yes, the plays, and the all-pervasive sense that everybody in the building feels a bit betrayed by Tony, yet their utterly mindless worship of the holy church of theatre and their dogmatic belief in it will somehow cleanse them. It's difficult to know whether to laugh or cry with this mob. Perhaps I'm the wrong man in the wrong place, but, fuck it all, my attitude is badass. We have been in development hell for too long. We deserve a promotion upstairs.

We've had a few days to prepare, and now the invited audience begins to file in. For 15 minutes there is a warm genial buzz in the air as people take their seats. The atmosphere of jubilant anticipation is only interrupted by the arrival of Graham Mustard. The happy hum of the throng quickly turns to silence as only it can when there's a wanker in the room. The wanker moves quickly and stealthily like an oily eel through the auditorium, and is it my imagination or has Graham Mustard got an eye-patch on and is he leading his monkeys, Grahams Marx and Coldplay, along by a piece of string like a couple of blind mice? It must be my imagination. Graham Mustard sits in the middle of the front row of seats, three foot from the stage, and looks at the floor. He will continue to stare out the floor for the next two hours. The floor will ultimately win.

Graham Director signals for silence, and for a few seconds

I hold my breath – then the show begins.[53] The opening 'Overture' is set at Brighton racetrack in the early 60s – it's a long and menacing piece and the actors are palpably nervous, but when they start getting into the choreographed moves (really, choreography) then the nerves begin to evaporate. After ten hard minutes the set piece is up and we win some good applause. Now the actors have to duke it out to get through to the other side of Act One, which ends with a 'show stopper' of a number called 'Dandification': the protagonist Guy Pollard (Hoogstraten) goes through a lairy dance routine at a funeral, before breaking into a soft-shoe shuffle and singing, 'This is the brand new age of violence, pretty violence, and style . . .' The actors hit the song hard – and win. 'Dandification', this 'big number', closes the first act to ecstatic applause. The audience are willing us on. Graham Mustard continues his battle with the floor.

Act Two has been set up for laughs and the gambit pays off: the audience, and this is an audience used to 'the theatre', are digging what they see and, y'know, laughing. Right-wing caricatures ham it up on stage – a bit of Alan Clark here, a bit of Jimmy Goldsmith and John Aspinall there, and of course the inevitable pop-ups from Lord Lucan. It's a fucking

[53] Over the course of the next three paragraphs I have refrained from giving a full breakdown of the plot of the show – it is, ahem, a theatrical 'piece', so by definition is quite 'plotty'. On the page this just will not translate. In Chapter 24 I have included a transcript of what is referred to elsewhere in this book as 'a couple of tatty pieces of coffee-stained A4 paper'. I have also omitted most *Property* song titles for reasons of clarity. There were over 20 songs written for the musical.

hoot. Act Three is a barnstormer, comprising entirely a ridiculous 15-minute epic number called 'Building for Britain in the 70s': 'Get your foot . . . out the door . . . with your modern and affordable homes for all,' sings Guy Pollard, ludicrously, to a 'rival' property developer, all over a mental orthodox glam stomp, based around Gary Glitter's 'Hello, Hello, I'm Back Again'. It's idiotic, and it brings the house down – we've got enough applause in the bank to safely take this muthafucka home. The audience merrily trail out to get their intermission refreshments. Graham Mustard continues to stare at the floor.

No one mentions the wanker in the room. This whole show is starting to seem immense. How can one person be bigger than all this? I head back to my seat as the second half gets under way. My favourite scene, involving a duet between Lord Lucan and Guy Pollard, actually moves a girl in the audience to tears. Then it happens. The unthinkable. Just as the fourth act is coming to a close, Pollard utters his line:

'I've met the man in the street – and he's a cunt.'[54]

The audience laugh. Then Graham Mustard looks up. And laughs. Out of the corner of my eye I see Grahams Marx and Coldplay look at each other – the very foundations of their silly little world crumbling. Then it becomes obvious: it's not that weird, it's the one thing that Führer Mustard can relate to, because when he has to come down from the

[54] A line once uttered in an interview by Sid Vicious. Perhaps Sid's one great contribution.

Eagle's Nest, after a long, hard day's autocracy, he does have to breathe the same air as the man in the street, and yes, he thinks that the man in the street is a cunt. Hahahaha. Graham Mustard is just like me – we are cut from the same cloth (a brown shirt?), we are two peas in the same pod (a bunker in Berlin?). Graham Mustard is clearly a man after my own heart – wants to reinstate a three-tier class system and put the working classes back into service. Oh Graham, you and I could have been so good together, if only you had passed your City and Guilds in communications just like I did, and if only you hadn't sacrificed your inner fascist to the non-secular gods of the scaredy cat – yet ruthlessly ambitious–liberal arts guardians. It's all over in a flash, and before the audience have stopped laughing Graham Mustard averts his eyes and turns the corners of his mouth downwards.

One last act and one finale later and the battle with the floor is over, it has claimed another victim. From what I can tell – level of applause, amount of laughter, absence of yawning, no fatalities from boredom – I would say that *Property* has been a success. Strangely, someone else thinks so.

'It was fantastic,' gushes Graham Mustard, his comedy German accent briefly deserting him. 'Wonderful,' he enthuses, 'I really can't believe it.' Obviously there is some ambiguity in this last statement (somewhat akin to the apocryphal theatrical after-show greeting 'Congratulations, you've done it again'), but then he continues, 'Let's meet up next week and discuss what happens next.' Graham

Mustard holds out his hand for me to shake and smiles for the second time in his life. He maybe even manages a nanosecond of eye contact. There is no surprise, however, when I make contact with his skin: his hand still feels like a bag of broken lizard bones. I chat with well-wishers and strangers from the audience, who assure me that the show cannot fail – remember, this is the theatre. Out of the corner of my eye I see Graham Marx listening intently to Graham Mustard. The actors, Simon, and I take our business to the alehouse, where Graham Marx is for once conspicuous by his absence.

Over the next week Simon Bent and I are super-confident; we spend the days waiting for Mustard's verdict, kicking round ideas. We are both keen on the Lord Lucan 'cameo' scenes in *Property* and come up with an idea for a whole Lucan musical – *Lucky*, the story about a gambler on the edge of a nervous breakdown who wanders into the 'Lucky Turf Accountants', only to find that he has stepped into a portal for World War Two fighter pilots who have disappeared, missing explorers, and of course Lord Lucan.

'Lucky – unlucky in love
Lucky – unlucky in cards'

goes the theme song – perhaps we have been working too hard.

'Graham Mustard hates the show,' says Graham Coldplay, one week later, somewhat, but not entirely, forlornly. Graham Marx, who also looks somewhat, but not entirely, forlorn, adds, 'He doesn't think it's political enough.' By this he means it is not about the Iraq war.

The two Grahams shuffle whatever bits of paper they have to hand, and Graham Coldplay turns towards his computer screen and pretends to attend to something urgent. If Graham Marx had a computer to hand he would do the same. *Never mind, Graham Marx, you have a whole lifetime ahead of you where you can pretend to attend to something urgent. I have no doubt that there will be many more time-wasting theatre workshops in the future that will require your scrutiny. Soon we will be out of your life.* Sooner than I think. Apparently.

'*Property* is no longer a National Theatre concern,' says Graham Coldplay. The only thing he omits to say is 'There's the door, there's the handle – you know how to use it.' I get up and politely shake hands with the Grahams. *There's the door. There's the handle. I know how to use it*, I think to myself. That musical about Lord Lucan will just have to wait, I guess.

I catch an empty lunchtime tube train home. I can't quite get my head around the fact that two years' work has come to nothing. The only thing I can think about is my strange craving for scrambled eggs. I get off at my stop and buy eggs. I return home to find my wife Siân lying in bed feeling unwell. She asks me how the meeting went, so I tell her the bad news. There's a programme on about Fred Dibnah, the master chimney exploder, that I want to watch; he was good at blowing up chimneys was Fred. I tell my wife I have to make scrambled eggs and that I need to watch the Dibnah show.

30

Sam the Dead Cat's recipe for scrambled eggs

November 2005. Dead cat back from the future.
Post Everything. 2 eggs, a little olive oil or butter, 1 tin of anchovies, 1 talking cat.

As I reach into the cupboard to get a saucepan to scramble the eggs in, I hear a blood-curdling animal cry.

'Wheeaah,' shrieks the cat.

'Jesus, Sam, you frightened the life out of me. How did you get in that cupboard?'

'Of all the stupid questions to ask a talking cat,' retorts Sam the Bad Cat, not unreasonably.

'Anyway, how have you been?'

'All in good time,' says Sam. 'First of all, you look like you need help making those scrambled eggs, let me show you how. The first rule of good scrambled eggs is to use butter instead of milk. Melt the butter – or olive oil – until it liquidises and then add the secret ingredient,' the mental cat gastronaut winks at me and holds out a paw clutching a tin of anchovies.

'I'll open those for you,' I say, as Sam carries on his cookery lecture.

'Now, keeping the pan on a low heat – you can gently stir in a couple of anchovies, remember tinned are best, you are essentially using these little fish as a superior stock substitute.'

'That's interesting,' I say, genuinely interested.

'Now, when the anchovies have melted, it's time to add the eggs and stir. Oh, and one thing, it's very important to cook eggs on a low heat. Eggs like to be cooked on low heat. Got that? Now repeat after me. What do eggs like?'

'To be cooked on a low heat,' I parrot back. 'So, Sam the Bad Cat, where have you been?' I ask as I stir the eggy mixture around the pan.

'I've been hanging out in the future, 2011 actually, where I used up the last of my nine lives – got ripped to pieces by a fox, terrible business.'

'Gosh, I'm really sorry to hear that, Sam', I say sadly. 'I've had a bad day as well.'

'I know,' says Sam the Dead Cat. ' I'm afraid there's some more bad shit around the corner.' Just as I'm about to press the moggie on this impending doom he changes the subject.

'Right, let's eat scrambly eggys,' squeaks the dead pussy.

*

'The anchovies are certainly an excellent addition,' I say, finishing up my plate of scrambled eggs.

'Mmmm, mmm,' confirms Sam. 'Look, I've got to go now, it's been good to see you an' all, but I'm on borrowed time, my cat lives are all used up and I aint gonna stick around here talking shit with you. Oh, talk to your wife, she has something good to tell you.' I get up from the table and head towards the kitchen door, I turn around to say ta ta to Sam, but he's gone. Goodbye Sam the Dead Cat.

I go into the other room. Siân has some news for me – she is pregnant. It's been an emotional day.

31

Dead honest independent record label run by people who are in no way delusional fantasists

July 2005–January 2006. Bad vibes, good vibes, worse vibes. Post Everything. Thankfully London Underground bombings do not unduly affect series seven of Big Brother. *In August, Robin Cook and Mo Mowlam die. Gary Glitter is arrested at his home in Vung Tau, Vietnam, and charged with molesting two underage girls. Hut Records, by now operating from the ground floor of the Virgin Records mansion, finally closes down. Primal Scream still going strong.*

Post Everything, the music business of the 1950s, 1960s, 1970s, 1980s, and 1990s really is a goner. Just like the colliery pits, they're gradually shutting the whole gaff down. Artist Antony Gormley's most famous folly, *The Angel of the North*, spreads her wings over a disused mine shaft in Tyneside

(Northshire). Southshire never really got it on with a convincing retort,[55] but perhaps the ideal location for the *Angel of the South* will be on the ruins of Abbey Road Studios, NW6. The problem lies in trying to restore an equilibrium. Forget it; if it ain't broken don't try to fix it – and if it *is* broken then don't try to fix it. Sometimes things are just fucked for ever. For 50 years the music biz shaped the backbone of popular culture – and provided a weirdly corrupt playpen for some lucky (and unlucky) boys and girls. Fabulous artists, fabulous chancers, n'er do wells and n'er do nothings. Genius, idiot, visionary, moron, saint, and devil – all classes, Johnny B. Goode and Johnny Too Bad, the wild, the willing, the innocent, murderers, and victims. For 50 years all comers were welcome to try their hand. But the music industry of old has gone now so don't try to restore it. The Golden Age of Rock 'n' Roll (1955–2005) will in time be looked upon as a blip in history. I was lucky enough to grab a last slice of the cake during the era of that blip. Future generations will make their own luck. Raise a glass to the death of the music industry. Let it bleed, let it die, good riddance.

When *Property* receives its lethal injection from the National Theatre my body goes into reflex mode – any money I have is dwindling from the two years spent working on the musical. My wife and I have a baby on the way. I need to act fast. I have two choices: hit the wall and

[55] So far a 40-foot 'Willow Man' in Somerset, and an ongoing plan for a £2 million sculpture of a white horse in Ebbsfleet, Kent.

try to claw my way through, or just hit the wall. I choose the former. My publishers, BMG, bankroll me to go into the studio for a marathon six weeks, where I decide to record the songs I wrote at the end of the *Property* workshops – the ones I'd hoped I wouldn't immediately need but now do. I also elect to record the entire *Property* soundtrack/score. If only for posterity. There have been a few half-hearted attempts to get *Property* up and running since November but all to no avail. The best thing to do is forget about it – for now. One musical, there for the taking. Goodbye cruel theatrical world. Manager Charlie has also gone. Tired out of rock 'n' roll. Goodbye cruel rock 'n' roll world. *Property* was not quite the new chapter I had hoped for.

Our son is born in July 2005. My former record label, EMI, celebrate by putting out a three-CD compilation, which I name *Luke Haines Is Dead*. I spend months trawling through the sacred archives at Abbey Road searching out musty old master tapes. The last time I was here was to record *After Murder Park*. Then, when my son is born, good things seem to happen: a new management company steps up and a couple of record labels start to show interest in the recordings that I made alongside *Property*. After weighing up my options I elect to license the recordings to a company called Dead Honest Independent Record Label Run by People Who Are Not in Any Way Delusional Fantasists (DHIRLRBPWANIAWDF). I am starting again.

Brendan O'Malley runs DHIRLRBPWANIAWDF. O'Malley is a charmer, a chancer, a flatterer, and as it turns out a very distant stranger to all things truthful. Remember all that stuff in my first book *Bad Vibes: Britpop and My Part in Its Downfall*, about Clive Solomon and Fire Records? (Come on, the 'dream sequence' with Jarvis in the loincloth chucking spears around was *inspired*.) Remember all the griping about 'indie svengalis' and lousy contracts? Hell, I even have a bit of a whine about the perceived wisdom on independent labels in this very tome. Well, in January 2006, I seem to have forgotten all of that, when I sign over the recordings for what will become the *Off My Rocker at the Art School Bop*[56] album over to Brendan O'Malley and the Dead Honest Independent Record Label Run by People Who Are Not in Any Way Delusional Fantasists. What I haven't noticed is that the Dead Honest Independent Record Label Run by People Who Are Not in Any Way Delusional Fantasists are not actually called the DHIRLRBPWANIAWDF. They are actually called Please Wake Me Up from This Nightmare Records. Starting again will not be so easy.

[56] *Off My Rocker at the Art School Bop* is eventually released a year after these events on an entirely different label.

Epilogue:

Between Bob Hope and no hope

March 2006. I am speaking to my 'label boss', Brendan O' Malley, on the phone. He breaks down. Brendan O' Malley, who with his flinty Irish girlfriend Shona runs Please Wake Me Up from This Nightmare Records, owes me £10,000. I don't mean to 'reduce him to tears' or any such macho crap, I just calmly tell him what I think: that he is a fucking liar. If I was a psychologist I would hazard a diagnosis that Brendan O'Malley is a compulsive liar who has a pathological problem with telling the truth. But I am not a psychologist so I cannot say this. I am merely a borassic man. Brendan has told me so much horse shit over the last few months that he can no longer cover his tracks. It's embarrassing: the motherfucker has tied himself up in so many delusions that he has effectively made a straitjacket for himself. Then it happens, oh Christ, does it happen – the floodgates open and he's blubbing into the receiver, a grown man in his late thirties sobbing like a chastened child. I feel sorry for the cunt, whilst at the same time suspecting that I have just been lured into another delaying tactic. I tell him that I will give him until Monday to get his act together and pay me the money that he owes me. He gathers himself a little and promises me he will do the right thing. I put down the telephone and assess that my chances of getting Brendan O'Malley to cough up lie approximately between Bob Hope and no hope.

This nonsense has been going on since January, when I first signed a licensing deal with PWMUFTN Records. Behind every craven idiot man is a craven idiot woman. Whenever I telephone O'Malley to catch up with the latest excuses, I can hear Shona in the background, pushing and prompting. Advance on signature. Advance. On. Signature. Well, I autographed the contract three months ago and . . . nothing, just miserable lie after miserable lie.

The deadline of midday Monday passes with stomach-churning predictability. I remain pot-less. I seethe, I rage, and I scream blue murder as I attack the defenceless living room table with a small screwdriver. Brendan O'Malley, you and your girlfriend/wife/sister/mother (whatever the hell she is) have fucking crossed me, and I will take my revenge. The last thing I hear as I slam the front door is the frightened cries of my eight-month-old son, who is being comforted in my wife's arms. Daddy is about to go postal.

Pram in the hallway, art out the door is how the old maxim bred cliché goes (though perhaps internet in the corner, art out the door would be more accurate). Maybe? But this all hangs upon the notion that art is important. It is not, at least not half as important as any artist will have you believe. It is just something to paper over the cracks. It doesn't matter what I or you think. Art is endless, it will go on for ever.

I've been here before, I've seen off many a record company bozo in my time. Ten labels in almost 20 years. There's a rule that any music business lawyer will tell you (for a fee) that during your 'career' you are allowed to sign one bad contract. By this reckoning (a) my 'career' is over, and (b) I have just doubled my bad-contract quota.

I pound down Elgin Avenue towards O'Malley's HQ. My chest is heaving, but every step closer to my quarry is just a step nearer to no-man's-land. However hurt, betrayed, and – like some dunce who just got off the frigging boat – conned I feel by O'Malley, I know that I must walk away from this stinking mess. I can only think of my son crying. I pace up and down outside Brendan's lair, three times for good measure, and out of respect for my old self, who would have at least kicked the door in and at worst yelled some unspeakable threats (that I wouldn't have had the chops to carry out) within a hair's breadth of Brendan's quivering face. But right now, the only thing I'm going to do is swallow my pride. Soon I'll be 40, in the century that I will die in. I turn on my heels and head back towards the tube station, back home to Siân and my son, to start again. Besides, revenge is a dish best served cold.

Further reading

The following are referenced either obliquely or explicitly in the text, and may be of some interest:

Brothers of the Head / Where the Lines Converge – Brian Aldiss. Conjoined twins form a band. Forget about the movie, stick with this 1978 novella. See also *The Silent Twins*.

Somebody's Son, Somebody's Husband – Gordon Burn.

There's a Riot Going On – Peter Doggett. Amerikkka, the counterculture, and all that . . .

The Pepsi Cola Addict – June Gibbons. Malibu teen Preston Wildey King hates Coke but lurvves Pepsi. Preston's permanent and improbable cola high lead him to crime and reform school, where he takes his own life by washing down a lethal dose of barbiturates with . . . Pepsi Cola.

Disco Mania – Jennifer Gibbons. Disco kids are incited into psychotic ultra-violence on the dance floor by terrifying new dance beats.

The Pugilist – Jennifer Gibbons. A family dog is killed to provide a transplantable heart for a dying child. Hmmm, er, right on. Both *The Pepsi Cola Addict* and *Disco Mania* were published in small numbers in the US. They are of course rarer than a joke in *Mojo* magazine. As for the one about the dog . . .

England Made Me – Graham Greene.

Art Strike Papers – Stewart Home. Original Pop Strike idea.

Assault on Culture – Stewart Home.

Neoism, Plagiarism and Praxis – Stewart Home.

Memphis Underground – Stewart Home. Contains S. Home's thoughts on First National Pop Strike.

The Game of War: The Life and Death of Guy Debord – Andrew Hussey.

Christie Malry's Own Double-Entry – B. S. Johnson.

The Unfortunates – B. S. Johnson.

Words and Music – Paul Morley. Morley has a bit of a think about Kylie.

Red Riding Quartet– David Peace.

The Gamblers: John Aspinall, James Goldsmith and the Murder of Lord Lucan – John Pearson.

All the Devils Are Here – David Seabrook.

Jack of Jumps – David Seabrook. The Jack the Stripper murders.

The Silent Twins – Marjorie Wallace. Biography of June and Jennifer Gibbons.

Theorem of the Moron – Dr Karl Wilkie. Very much out of print. Unlikely to be back in print.

The Occult – Colin Wilson. Spook compendium well thumbed by every 70s schoolboy.

Further listening

Some music references, such as the reggae artists referred to in Chapter 2, and the MC5 footnote in Chapter 22, I have left within the text. Others mentioned in passing I have chosen to expand upon here.

Black Sabbath – *Black Sabbath* (1970), *Paranoid* (1970), *Master of Reality* (1971), *Volume Four* (1972), *Sabbath Bloody Sabbath* (1973), *Sabotage* (1975). Sabbath's first five albums on the Vertigo label are only just beginning to be understood by serious rock critics, not that that ever mattered. Ozzy's Midlands death trip culminates in 1975's *Sabotage*. From the sleeve onwards one of the strangest records ever made. Lyrics often written by Brummie shaman Terry 'Geezer' Butler. Now if we could just forget about that bloody TV show, those bloody offspring, and that damned woman.

British Lions – After Ian Hunter left Mott the Hoople, there was Mott, after Mott there was British Lions, who released one last great single, 'International Heroes' (1979). Essential Mott the Hoople albums, in case you are in any doubt: *Brain Capers* (1971), *All the Young Dudes* (1972), *Mott* (1973), *The Hoople* (1974). Ian Hunter solo albums: *Ian Hunter* (1975), *All American Alien Boy* (1976), *You're Never Alone with a Schizophrenic* (1979). *All American Alien Boy* is perhaps the under-appreciated jewel – even, it seems, by Hunter. Up there with, and not dissimilar to, Dave's *Young Americans*.

The Doors – Always the cue for a discourse on the death of rock. There is wheat and there is chaff. If you don't dig Jim you are chaff. There are men and there are little boys. Once again, if you don't 'get' The Morrison, I know which one you are. If there's no love for the Doors then you ain't welcome round these parts. There's a special place for blustering bad drunken poetry, leather trousers, and priapic shamans. That place is called rock 'n' roll. For the Doors as 'existentialist bar band' (Jim's own brilliant description) go for *Morrison Hotel/Hard Rock Café* (1970) and *Rock Is Dead* (drunken jam –1969). Chapter 9 of this book dabbles in psycho-acoustics, and Chapter 20 makes with the punk rules and Post Everything non-rules. Right now I need to blow a little pre-irony rock 'n' roll up yer ass. In order for rock 'n' roll to be fully accepted, mythology must remain intact. Rules or no rules – rock is Rosicrucian text. Sacrosanct. 'Weren't the 90s great,' goes my own line in 'The Rubettes'. I am guilty of hiding behind the ironic statement. Do you think that any of those Britpop bands gave a fuck about anything other than their own ambition? For my generation was it anything more than one big fucking laugh? Sure the rock 'n' roll heart of 90s rock was consumed with angst, Kurt, Radiohead, and any US alt rock grunt you care to mention, but much of that angst was born out of needless self-hatred at the, *gasp*, thought of being a corporate sellout. Jeez Louise, gimme a break, come on muthafuckas it's not exactly David Crosby at Monterey Pop pontificating on who killed JFK, it's not Arlo Guthrie at Woodstock marvelling at the fact that the interstate freeway is closed, and it ain't Sly Stone threatening to quit the scene 'cos he's getting so much fucking heat from the Black Panthers. Yep, irony existed before the 80s/90s with Bowie and, gulp, Zappa (see *Uncle Meat* entry in this chapter), but in the kingdom of irony the lizard cannot be king – unless the lizard king takes to wearing a fucking comedy headband, and that shit ain't never gonna fly. Face it, brothers and sisters, a rock 'n' roll pantheon without Jim Morrison would be a dismal place. So when Jimbo stepped into that bath, the Doors not only lost their lead singer – rock lost its licence to commune with dead Indians whilst keeping a straight face, and that, people, is a tragedy.

David Essex – In '75 all girls were Essex girls, and the real king of pop had several careers: hitmaker, movie star – in two of the best British movies about rock 'n' roll ever made – and as an avant-garde trailblazer with the following smash hit singles: 'Rock On' (1973), 'Lamplight' (1973), 'Streetfight' (1974), and *Stardust* (1974).

Peter Hammill – *Nadir's Big Chance* (1975). Hammill

invokes his inner teenage moron in the guise of 16-year-old Rikki Nadir. Good album.

Kiss – Got to make room for a little Kiss in your heart. Just as Sabbath have the problem of *The Osbournes* TV show, with Kiss there is always going to be the problem of Gene Simmons. Never mind, listen to *Destroyer* (1976) enough and, whilst you'll never actually like Gene, the music's good enough to pretend that 'the Demon' just ain't there. 'Detroit Rock City', 'Beth', and the track that the Clash secretly based their entire second album upon: 'Kings of the Night-Time World'.

John Lennon Plastic Ono Band – In a footnote to Chapter 8, 'Pop music is wasted on the young', I describe Lennon/Ono's *Some Time in New York City* (1972) as 'disastrous'. Well, yes, in terms of commercial and critical reception, but in many ways *STINYC* is Lennon's defining artistic/radical statement; whilst there's no denying the avant-garde chops of the no-wave jazz fuck 'Cambridge 1969', from the Lennons' grim *Life with the Lions* album, by '72, the former Beatle was actively hanging out with real-deal countercultural revolutionaries Jerry Rubin and Abbie Hoffman, soaking it all up and then letting it all seep out on *STINYC*. Apart from that bloke out of Slade 2 threatening to marry Rose West, there really is no modern equivalent of a contemporary pan-global superstar going as fabulously off message as John Lennon did after the Beatles. Plus, 'Woman Is the Nigger of the World', 'Attica State', and 'New York City' rock hard (and there's nothing too much wrong with having a 15-minute live version of Yoko's signature tune 'Don't Worry

Kyoko (Mummy's Only Looking for Her Hand in the Snow)'). The first Plastic Ono Band's single, 'Give Peace a Chance', bore the legend, 'You Are the Plastic Ono Band'. Interesting that much of Lennon's infinitely superior post-Beatles output has almost been reduced to the 'Imagine' brand/caricature.

Motörhead – *Motörhead* (1977), *Overkill* (1979), *Bomber* (1979). On being booted out of Hawkwind, after a botched amphetamine bust in Toronto, 'bass strangler' Lemmy already had his speed-king biker image well sorted. *Motörhead* featured a few numbers written for his old band. It took *Overkill* and *Bomber* to perfect the Motörhead aesthetic. By the time of *Ace of Spades,* it was almost self-parody, but who the hell cares when the public are buying in droves. As Lemmy went stratospheric in 1980, his old band Hawkwind had had their best. Their entire UA catalogue is essential – Pink Floyd with *no educashun: In Search of Space* (1971), *Doremi Fasol Latido* (1972), *Space Ritual* (1973), advertised at the time as '90 minutes of brain damage', and *Hall of the Mountain Grill* (1974), featuring the proto-Pistols 'Psychedelic Warlords'. When 'Space Poet' in residence Robert Calvert became lead singer and main lyricist in 1976, Hawkwind metamorphosed almost unrecognisably. *Hawklords – 25 Years On* (1978) may be their finest half-hour, a concept album about 'Pan Transcendental Industries Inc', a corporation which clips the wings off angels to make car doors. For the late Bob Calvert, if there was a line to toe, then he didn't know where it was. His 1974 solo album *Captain Lockheed and the Starfighters* was another concept piece, this time about the post-war Luftwaffe buying up crocked bombers from the American air force. Featuring spoken word and skits from Calvert and Viv Stanshall, and propulsive early-sevs prime space rock from the rest of the 'wind. And Brian Eno. We live in paltry times, children, we live in paltry times.

Yoko Ono – *Plastic Ono Band* (1970), *Fly* (1971), *Approximately Infinite Universe* (1973). Yoko's Plastic Ono Band output often ran concurrently with or as a counterpoint to Lennon's outpourings. As has often been written, a precursor to early Public Image Ltd – not just sonically but in the way that the Plastic Ono Band marketed themselves as a kind of avant-garde corporation just like PiL. *Plastic Ono Band*, released simultaneously with Lennon's same titled though known as 'the primal scream album', is the *real* primal scream album. Blood-curdling banshee howls over hard-bop knuckle-headed free-rock jamming. Ringo's there, but sadly George isn't. This is what the Beatles could have sounded like if they'd carried on after sad Mac hopped off.

Scritti Politti – *Anomie and Bonhomie* (1999). Never cared much for their early, skeletal Marxist doodles, or even the early-80s chart-bothering pop, but this late-90s expensive-sounding production was never off the turntable. Big influence on *The Oliver Twist Manifesto*.

Status Quo – *Ma Kelly's Greasy Spoon* (1970), *Dog of Two Head* (1971), *Piledriver* (1972), and their 1976 masterpiece, *Blue for You*. It was only after the *Whatever You Want* (1979) album that Quo got treated as some kind of joke. Up until then they could do no wrong. The real sound of the 70s.

For a career revamp, I'd suggest one more album of no-nonsense, heads-down shuffle boogie. Careful with the cover versions and, most importantly, get Steve Albini in to 'produce'.

Uncle Meat – Note that this entry is for the album rather than the artist, and I wouldn't advise that you go there, really I wouldn't. But if you must then opt for 1968's *Uncle Meat*. You won't need to trawl through any more of Zappa's 'hefty' back catalogue – *Uncle Meat* (the soundtrack to an unfinished and barely comprehensible movie) has all the obsessions and ticks on one sprawling mess of genius (did I really just write 'genius' goddamnit?) album. The puerile song titles, the unfunny 'humour', maddening spastic jazz, irritating muso superiority, casual misogyny, and the laboured and horribly mouldy in-joke of Suzy Creamcheese. In spite of all these fatal flaws *Uncle Meat* is a fucking great album. Frank does not give a shit.

Acknowledgements

Thank you to Siân, my agent Clare Conville and all at Conville and Walsh. My editor Jason Arthur and all at William Heinemann and Windmill Books. Thanks also to John Moore, Sarah Nixey, Charlie Inskip, and David Boyd.